Apple Pro Training Series
Shake 4

Marco Paolini

Apple
Certified

Apple Pro Training Series: Shake 4
Marco Paolini
Copyright © 2006 by Marco Paolini

Published by Peachpit Press. For information on Peachpit Press books, contact:

Peachpit Press
1249 Eighth Street
Berkeley, CA 94710
(510) 524-2178
Fax: (510) 524-2221
http://www.peachpit.com
To report errors, please send a note to errata@peachpit.com.
Peachpit Press is a division of Pearson Education.

Series Editor: Serena Herr
Managing Editor: Kristin Kalning
Editors: Anita Dennis, William Rodarmor
Production Editor: Laurie Stewart, Happenstance Type-O-Rama
Copy Editors: Hon Walker, Karen Seriguchi
Apple Reviewer: Dion Scoppettuolo
Technical Reviewer: Ron Ganbar
Compositor: Robin Kibby, Happenstance Type-O-Rama
Indexer: Jack Lewis
Interior and Cover Design: Frances Baca
Cover Art Direction: Charlene Charles-Will
Cover Illustration: Alicia Buelow
Cover Production: George Mattingly / GMD

ISBN 0-321-25609-3
9 8 7 6 5 4 3
Printed and bound in the United States of America

To who else—Mom and Dad

Acknowledgments When I was asked to write this book, I severely underestimated the time it would take to accomplish the task. To the responsible parties, thank you for getting me into this; I hope one day to return the favor. To everybody who had to put up with me throughout the writing of this book, I apologize. To those who kept me on track and guided me along the way, thanks.

Patty Montesion Thanks for giving me the opportunity to write this book and believing in me.

Peter Warner Thanks for allowing me to adapt some of your tutorials and documentation.

Anita Dennis and Kristin Kalning Thanks for hunting down and obtaining permission for all of the high-quality footage. It elevated the book from being merely good to truly great.

Peachpit Press Thanks to the entire team at Peachpit Press who did all of the thankless, behind-the-scenes production of this book.

My wife and kids Thanks for putting up with me.

Contents at a Glance

Table of Contents

Getting Started

The leading compositing system for feature film effects, Shake from Apple is a high-speed compositing software application optimized for high-resolution visual effects. Designed for quality, flexibility, and efficiency, Shake has quickly become the leading compositing choice for feature films. Since its debut in 1998, Shake has been used in every film that has won the Academy Award for Best Visual Effects.

Shake 4 now offers a host of new features that give you the highest-quality output for film and video, so you can create convincing, photo-realistic visual effects on a desktop. It is the only compositing software with a complete tool set for both single artists and visual effects facilities. With 3D MultiPlane compositing, 32-bit Keylight and Primatte keying, Optical Flow image processing, Final Cut Pro 5 integration, and an open, extensible scripting language, Shake 4 includes the tools required for sophisticated film and television visual effects.

About Apple Pro Training Series

Apple Pro Training Series: Shake 4 is part of the official training series for Apple graphics, editing, and authoring software developed by experts in the field. The lessons are designed to let you learn at your own pace. If you're new to Shake, you'll appreciate being able to learn the fundamental concepts and features you'll need to master the program. If you've been using Shake for a while, you'll find that this book teaches many advanced features, including tips and techniques for using the latest version of the application.

Although each lesson provides step-by-step instructions for creating a specific project, there's room for exploration and experimentation. I recommend that you follow the book from start to finish, or at least complete the first seven chapters before jumping around haphazardly. Each lesson concludes with a review section summarizing what you've learned.

System Requirements

Before beginning to use *Apple Pro Training Series: Shake 4,* you should have a working knowledge of your computer and its operating system. Make sure that you know how to use the mouse and standard menus and commands, and also how to open, save, and close files. If you need to review these techniques, see the printed or online documentation included with your system.

Before you install Shake, make sure that your system meets the following requirements:

Macintosh Minimum System Requirements

▶ Power Mac G5; Power Mac G4 or PowerBook G4 with 1 GHz PowerPC G4 processor

▶ Mac OS X v10.3.9

▶ QuickTime 7.0

▶ 512MB of RAM

▶ 1GB of available disk space for caching and for temporary files

- ▶ AGP graphics card with 32MB of video memory and OpenGL hardware acceleration

- ▶ Display with 1280x1024-pixel resolution and 24-bit color

- ▶ Three-button mouse

- ▶ AJA Kona or Blackmagic DeckLink card (optional) for previewing composites on a broadcast video monitor

Installing Shake

The DVD accompanying this book contains a trial version of Shake 4 that includes a free 30-day license. Use the following guidelines to install and start the application on a system running Macintosh OS X 10.3.9 or later.

> **NOTE** ▶ Shake requires you to use Mac OS X 10.3.9 or later. If you do not have at least Mac OS X 10.3.9, you need to install it on your system before you can run the application.

The trial version of Shake 4 has the following limitations:

- ▶ A 30-day license period.

- ▶ 40 nodes per project.

- ▶ Saving is disabled.

- ▶ Copy and paste are disabled.

- ▶ Undo is disabled.

> **NOTE** ▶ If your trial version of Shake crashes or freezes for some unknown reason during the course of one of your lessons, you can load a script from the Lessons folder using the File > Open Script command. Just remove the nodes that you haven't gotten to yet, and continue where you left off before the crash occurred.

Installation Steps

The Shake installation process will require you to obtain a serial number from the Apple Web site before you install the trial software. We recommend you close all applications before you begin the installation.

1   Using a Web browser, go to www.apple.com/shake/trial.

2   Follow the instructions to obtain a serial number, which will be emailed to you. After you receive the serial number, proceed to the next step.

3   Insert the *Apple Pro Training Series: Shake 4* DVD into your DVD drive.

4   Go to the Trial Software folder and copy the `Shake4.00.dmg` file to your desktop.

5   Double-click the `Shake4.00.dmg` file.

The Shake4.0 volume is created and a Shake4.0 window opens.

6   Double-click the Install Shake 4.0 Trial icon.

7   In the Install Shake window, follow the onscreen instructions.

8   When prompted, enter the serial number you obtained from the Web site in step 2.

Destination Options

In the Select Destination dialog, installation is available only on partitions with Mac OS X 10.3.9 or later. By default, Shake is installed in the Applications folder on your hard drive. Although the Applications folder is the recommended folder, you can move Shake to a different folder.

Installation Options

In the Installation Type dialog, select one of the following installation options:

▶   Upgrade—Performs an Easy Install, which includes Shake and the documentation, but no tutorial images.

▶   Customize—Gives you the option to install Shake and the documentation, only the tutorial images, or Shake and the documentation with the tutorial images.

Shake Folder Contents

When Shake is installed, four icons appear in the Shake folder: Shake, shkqtv, shkv, and a doc folder. The Shake icon represents the Shake application, and it can be placed in the Dock. The shkv icon represents the Shake Viewer application (the flipbook player). You cannot launch the Shake Viewer application outside of Shake. When you create a flipbook in Shake, the Shake Viewer is launched automatically and the shkv icon appears in the Dock.

> **NOTE** ▶ All of the Shake files are stored within the application. To view the Shake package contents, Control- or right-click the Shake icon and choose Show Package Contents.

Copying the Shake Lesson Files

The *Apple Pro Training Series: Shake 4* DVD includes folders containing all the electronic files for the lessons. Each lesson has its own folder. You must install these folders on your hard drive to use the files for the lessons. To save room on your drive, you can install the folders for each lesson as you need them.

Installing the Shake Lesson Files

1   Insert the *Apple Pro Training Series: Shake 4* DVD into your DVD drive.

2   Create a folder on your hard drive and name it Shake Lessons.

3   Drag the Lessons folder from the DVD into the Shake Lessons folder on your hard drive.

Resources

This book is not meant to replace the documentation that comes with the program. Only the commands used in the lessons will be explained on these pages. For comprehensive information about program features, refer to these resources:

▶   The Shake User Manual—Accessed through the Shake Help menu, the Reference Guide contains a complete description of all features.

▶   Tutorials—The Shake Help menu includes a useful set of tutorials.

▶   The Apple Web site—You can view the Web site by choosing Help > Shake on the Web if you have a connection to the World Wide Web, or go to www.apple.com/shake.

Apple Pro Certification

The Apple Pro Training and Certification Program is designed to keep you at the forefront of Apple's digital media technology while giving you a competitive edge in today's ever-changing job market. Whether you're an editor, graphic designer, sound designer, special effects artist, or teacher, these training tools are meant to help you expand your skills.

Upon completing the course material in this book, you can become an Apple Pro by taking the certification exam at an Apple Authorized Training Center. Certification is offered in Final Cut Pro 5 (two levels), Motion 2, DVD Studio Pro 4, Logic Pro 7, Soundtrack Pro, and Shake 4. Successful certification as an Apple Pro gives you official recognition of your knowledge of Apple's professional applications while allowing you to market yourself to employers and clients as a skilled, pro-level user of Apple products.

To find an Apple Authorized Training Center near you, go to www.apple.com/software/pro/training.

For those who prefer to learn in an instructor-led setting, Apple also offers training courses at Apple Authorized Training Centers worldwide. These courses, which use the Apple Pro Training Series books as their curriculum, are taught by Apple Certified Trainers and balance concepts and lectures with hands-on labs and exercises. Apple Authorized Training Centers for Pro products have been carefully selected and have met Apple's highest standards in all areas, including facilities, instructors, course delivery, and infrastructure. The goal of the program is to offer Apple customers, from beginners to the most seasoned professionals, the highest-quality training experience.

1

The Shake Workflow

Shake is a collection of image manipulation engines, including those for compositing, color correcting, and warping. Each engine can be driven by a series of different commands called (interchangeably) *nodes, processes,* or *functions.* For example, Brightness is a node that changes the brightness of an image; Pan is a node that moves the image left and right or up and down. Each node usually has a series of parameters (or values) that can be adjusted. These nodes are connected to images and arranged in what is called a *process tree* because, well, it kind of looks like a tree.

The interesting thing about Shake is that the nodes and their parameters can be edited either in the graphical user interface (GUI) or from the command line in a Terminal window. It makes no difference to the composite how these nodes are executed from Shake, but each method has its advantages and disadvantages in terms of workflow. Shake's command-line functions are covered in Lesson 14.

Interface Workflow

▶ Images are read in from various folders.

	Name	Type	Size	Modified	Mode
📁	Lesson01	dir		22:52:35 Feb 15 2003	drwxrwxrwx
📁	Lesson02	dir		21:56:51 Feb 21 2003	drwxrwxrwx
📁	Lesson03	dir		22:53:40 Feb 15 2003	drwxrwxrwx
📁	Lesson04	dir		22:53:38 Feb 15 2003	drwxrwxrwx
📁	Lesson05	dir		18:46:13 May 30 2003	drwxrwxrwx
📁	Lesson06	dir		07:28:01 May 30 2003	drwxrwxrwx
📁	Lesson07	dir		15:18:29 May 08 2003	drwxrwxrwx
📁	Lesson08	dir		22:57:52 Feb 15 2003	drwxrwxrwx
📁	Lesson09	dir		11:08:41 Apr 02 2003	drwxrwxrwx
📁	Lesson10	dir		14:22:15 Mar 30 2004	drwxrwxrwx

▶ These images, as represented by thumbnails, are arranged in a process tree with color correctors, layering commands, keying, and other nodes connected to them to achieve the desired effect.

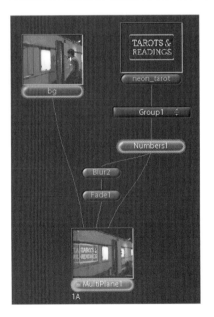

▶ The parameters of the nodes are tuned with interactive feedback in the Viewer.

▶ Once finished, a FileOut node is attached to the bottom of the process tree to tell Shake where to write the output image.

You can use as many FileOuts as you want, placed anywhere along the tree. In the full version of Shake, you can render from the interface by selecting the FileOut node and then choosing Render FileOut Nodes from the Render menu. In the trial version of Shake, you can render only by right-clicking a FileOut node and choosing one of the render options.

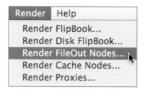

▶ Or you can save the tree as a text file called a *Shake script*.

```
○ ○ ○                    coke_marco_v2.shk
// Shake Beta v4.00.0525 - (c) Apple Computer, Inc. 1998-2005.  All Rights
Reserved.
// Apple, the Apple logo and Shake are trademarks of Apple Computer, Inc.,
registered in the U.S. and other countries.


SetTimeRange("1-110");
SetFieldRendering(0);
SetFps(24);
SetMotionBlur(1, 1, 0);
SetQuality(1);
SetUseProxy("Base");
SetProxyFilter("default");
SetPixelScale(1, 1);
SetUseProxyOnMissing(1);
SetDefaultWidth(720);
SetDefaultHeight(486);
SetDefaultBytes(1);
SetDefaultAspect(1);
SetDefaultViewerAspect(1);
SetMacroCheck(1);
SetTimecodeMode("24 FPS");

DefineProxyPath("No_Precomputed_Proxy", 1, 1, -1, "Auto", -1, 0, 0, "",1);
DefineProxyPath("No_Precomputed_Proxy", 0.5, 1, 1, "Auto", 0, 0, 1, "");
DefineProxyPath("No_Precomputed_Proxy", 0.25, 1, 1, "Auto", 0, 0, 2, "");
DefineProxyPath("No_Precomputed_Proxy", 0.1, 1, 1, "Auto", 0, 0, 3, "");
SetAudio("100W@E0000qFdsuHW962D19BOW0mWa06w7mCJ000000000008");

// Input nodes

bg = SFileIn("//Shark/Users/marco/Shake4/footage/coke/bg/bg.1-110#.iff",
```

▶ From the Terminal window or your own batch-rendering system, the
  effect is then rendered, and the output image is written to disk.

```
● ○ ○              Terminal — bash — 81x7
Last login: Sat Jul  9 19:30:37 on ttyp1
Welcome to Darwin!
shark:~ marco$ shake -exec coke.shk -vv
```

The Shake Interface

The time has come. You've just installed the Shake software; now you get to see
it in action. Before you start working with the various Shake processes, you
should become familiar with the Shake interface.

1   If you don't have a three-button mouse, go and buy one now.

NOTE ▶ You must have a three-button mouse to operate Shake properly.

2   Turn on your computer and monitor if they're not already on. The login
screen will appear momentarily.

3   Type your name and password at the login prompt.

4   Launch Shake by double-clicking the Shake icon located in your
Applications/Shake folder.

NOTE ▶ You may want to create an alias for the Shake icon on your
desktop.

After you launch Shake, you should see something that looks like this, but
without the silly numbers, which refer to the Shake workspaces:

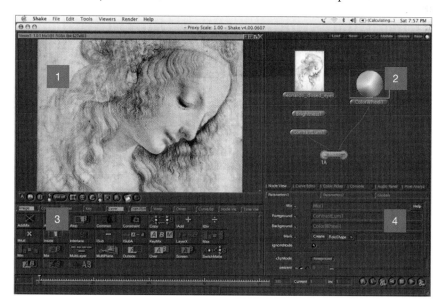

By default, Shake has four main workspaces:

1   The Viewer workspace

2   The Node workspace

3   The tool tabs

4   The Parameters workspace

   You can resize the four quadrants at any time by clicking and dragging the horizontal or vertical dividing lines of any two areas.

5   Click the dividing line between the Parameters workspace and the tool tabs and drag left and right to change the layout of the Shake interface.

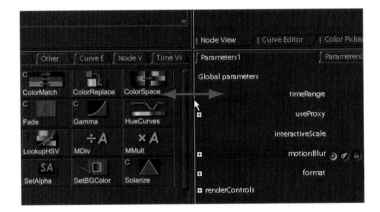

The Viewer Workspace

The Viewer workspace is where you create flipbooks to play back your images. This is also where your images and composites are interactively updated as you add nodes and change parameters. Here, you can look at the red, green, blue, or alpha components of an image. You can zoom in or out as well as create split screens to look at before-and-after views.

The Tool Tabs

The tool tabs allow you to choose what node you want to add to your process tree. Each node serves a particular function, such as color correcting, image filtering, or layering. The nodes are logically grouped into different tabs according to their functions.

The tool tabs include the following categories:

- ▶ Image
- ▶ Color
- ▶ Filter
- ▶ Key
- ▶ Layer
- ▶ Transform
- ▶ Warp
- ▶ Other
- ▶ Curve Editor
- ▶ Node View
- ▶ Time View

The Parameters Workspace

Adjustments made to a node's parameters take place inside the Parameters workspace. Clicking the right side of a node will place that node's particular set of controls into the Parameters workspace. You can adjust parameters by moving sliders, typing values, or entering expressions.

Global parameters are adjusted from within the Parameters workspace by clicking the Globals tab. These parameters affect the behavior of your entire effects setup, or what Shake refers to as a *script*, setting things like the time range and global motion blur controls. You can set many of these parameters in the command line, so you don't necessarily have to reset them each time you write out a script.

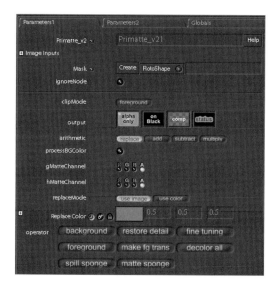

Primatte node loaded into Parameters workspace

The Node Workspace

In the Node workspace, you work with the many and varied process nodes.
This is where the magic happens. Clips and processes are combined, and
together they form a Shake script. The script, also known as a process tree,
can be saved, loaded, and reused later.

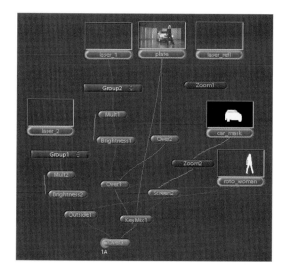

Color Picker

The Color Picker allows you to sample colors from the Viewer and transfer the color settings to applicable parameters. It can be found on the Color Picker tab in the Node workspace.

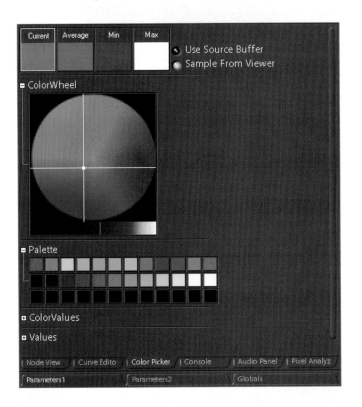

Pixel Analyzer

The Pixel Analyzer is an analysis tool used to find and compare different color values of an image. You can examine the minimum, average, current, and maximum pixel values on a selection or across an entire image. It's found on the Pixel Analyzer tab in the Node workspace.

Time View

The Time View tab shows a timeline of all clips and processes within a script. You can drag a clip to the left and right to change its start and end points in time, or drag its in and out points to change its duration.

Curve Editor

The Curve Editor allows you to create, see, and modify keyframes as well as animation curves and audio waveforms. You can change the curve type as well as its cycling mode. You can access the Curve Editor through the tool tabs as well as in the Node workspace.

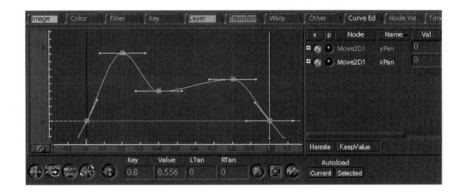

Audio Panel

The Audio Panel is used to read in AIFF or WAV files, mix them together, extract animation curves based on the audio frequency, manipulate the timing of the sound, and save the files again. Click the Audio Panel tab in the Node workspace to access it.

Other Interface Elements

▶ Pull-down menus—A series of pull-down menus is located at the top-left portion of the screen. Many common functions such as script loading and saving can be accessed through these menus.

▶ Render light—When the light is green, Shake isn't processing. When the light is red, it is. The cursor also changes to indicate processing.

▶ Load and Save—Clicking the Load and Save buttons (in the upper-right corner of the interface) calls up the File Browser to either load a script or save the current script with the same name. Remember that these buttons apply only to the loading and saving of scripts, not to the loading of media into Shake. To save a script under a new name, choose File > Save As, which will then prompt you for a script name. To reload the same script, choose File > Reload. This will reload the script that you see on the Shake title bar.

NOTE ▶ In the trial version of Shake, the capability to save scripts as well as to undo actions has been disabled.

▶ Infinite undo/redo—By saving changes into temporary files, Shake maintains infinite undo/redo. Not all changes are flagged as "undoable," though. For example, window sizes are not saved. The left arrow button performs an undo; the right arrow button does a redo.

You can also press Command-Z to undo and Command-Y to redo.

▶ Update buttons—The Update button allows you to choose how Shake will update the scene. There are three Update modes—Always, Manual, and Release—which you choose by clicking and holding the left mouse button on the button to the right of Update.

  ▶ Always—Shake always updates the scene when you change a parameter, including time.

  ▶ Manual—Shake never updates the scene, including time, until you click Update, the button on the left.

  ▶ Release—Shake updates the scene when you release the mouse after changing any parameter, including time.

▶ Proxy buttons—A proxy is a lower-resolution copy that you substitute for your high-resolution images so that you can work faster. The proxy buttons activate the use of proxy resolutions. When this is set to the Base position, it turns off the use of proxy images. Click and hold to choose a proxy resolution, or click to toggle between Base and the last-used proxy resolution.

▶   Title bar information—The title bar of the Shake window gives you current version data, as well as the current script name and the current proxy resolution.

/Users/marco/Shake4/footage/coke/coke_marco_v2.shk – Proxy Scale: 1.00 – Shake v4.00.0607

Contextual Help

Because most people will never read the Shake documentation, the Shake programmers have provided a contextual help window. As you pass the cursor over a button, the help window gives you a brief description of the button's function, as well as its hot key. The help information is located in a text window at the bottom center of the interface.

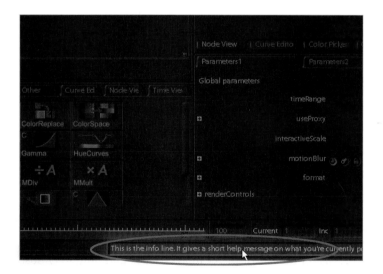

Node Help

Each Shake node has a Help button across from the node's name—the very first parameter listed on the Parameters tab. Click the Help button to open your current default browser and read an explanation of that particular node.

Online Documentation

For those rare souls who are actually interested in referring to the Shake documentation, you can access it by choosing Help > Shake User Manual. An Adobe PDF reader will open showing the Shake documentation.

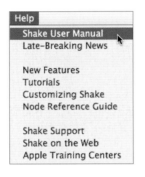

Importing Images and Sequences

Reading In an Image with the Browser

1   Drag the left mouse button along the tool tabs (Image, Color, Filter, and so on) to see all of the function nodes you can insert into a compositing, or process, tree.

    Notice that you can just drag the mouse; you don't have to click tabs individually to open them up.

2   To read in an image, you use the FileIn node in the Image tab. Click it, and it will launch the File Browser.

NOTE ▶ If you placed your Shake Lessons folder on a separate volume, open the Volumes folder from the File Browser to navigate to the destination volume.

The File Browser is used whenever you are loading and saving images or reading and writing scripts.

For this node, you will load the **sharks** clip, which is located inside the Lesson01 folder.

Browser Icons

At the top of the File Browser are seven icons, which are listed below.

Keystroke	Action
	Go up one folder level.
	Go back to the previous folder.
	Enable/disable relative file paths.

Keystroke	Action
	Bookmark the current folder.
	Create a new folder.
	Delete files/folders.
	Refresh a folder listing.

3 Double-click the Lesson01 folder.

When you enter the Lesson01 folder, you'll see one sequence listed.

4 Click **sharks.1-65#.iff** to select it.

5 Click OK to create a FileIn node in the Node View and load the image into the Viewer.

TIP ▸ When doing a FileIn, you can click OK to confirm and exit, or click Next to read in another file. Use Shift-click to select multiple files.

In the Viewer, you should see an image of a shark, and in the Node workspace, you should see one node named sharks.

6 Drag the mouse along the Time Bar at the bottom of the screen to see the frames update in the Viewer.

General Windowing

If you press the spacebar, you expand any workspace to fill the Shake screen.

1 Place the cursor over the Viewer and press the spacebar.

The Viewer workspace expands to the entire desktop.

2 Press the spacebar again to go back to the normal view.

Click the middle mouse button or Option-left-click to pan any workspace.

3 Pan the Viewer by Option-left-clicking.

Some workspaces, such as Parameters, only scroll up and down.

Using the Viewer

This section gets you up to speed on using the Viewer.

General Viewer Controls

Now that you have something to look at, I can explain a bit about the Viewer workspace. The Viewer workspace is the area where you view your images, create flipbooks, and evaluate your composites. You can create as many Viewers as you want, each dynamically updated in any channel you choose for any node you choose. This means that you can watch the behavior of a function as it modifies an alpha channel in both a Viewer looking at the alpha channel and a second Viewer looking at the composite itself.

The Viewers take up memory, so if you are rendering an image, you might want to close your higher-resolution Viewers. Additionally, the more Viewers you have active, the slower the display rate will be. If you are getting strange Viewer behavior, free up some memory by deleting the Viewers and create a new one by pressing the N key.

1   Experiment with some of the general window controls in the Viewer:

▶   Iconify the Viewer.

▶   Fit the Viewer to the image (or press Control-F).

▶   Fit the Viewer to the desktop (or press Shift-F).

▶   Close the window.

To reopen the Viewer for the sharks node, choose Viewer > New Viewer.

▶   Fit the image to the Viewer (or press F)—This may result in noninteger zooming; for example, zoomed not x2 but x2.01, which may cause inaccuracies in the display of the image due to the inherent rounding of pixel rows.

▶   Reset the Viewer zoom and pan to default (or press Home)—This centers and sets the zoom to a 1:1 ratio.

▶   Broadcast Monitor—When selected, the broadcast monitor mirrors the selected node (the node displayed in the Viewer). Before selecting this button, you should first choose your footage format from the Format parameter of the Globals tab of the Parameters workspace.

2   Drag the cursor while pressing the left mouse button in the image area to see X, Y, R, G, B, and alpha values in the help field and the title bar.

Viewer1: 1:1.0 NRiScript1@65 RGBA 8bit 720x363 X=285 Y=110 R=0.090 G=0.392 B=0.643 A=0.000

3   Toggle the Channel Viewer using the left mouse button.

The Channel Viewer toggles between the full-color image and the alpha channel. You can view the individual channels by first placing your cursor over the image area and pressing the R, G, B, A, and C keys to toggle between the red, green, blue, alpha, and color, or RGB, view planes. If you can't remember those five keystrokes, click and hold your left mouse button over the Channel Viewer to make your selection.

TIP ▶ Channel Viewer hot key: The 2 key cycles through the channels R, G, B, A, and RGB. Pressing 2 toggles forward and Shift-2 toggles backward. The cursor must be in the Viewer window.

4   Press N ("new" Viewer) when the cursor is over the Viewer to clone it.

5   Place the cursor over the Viewer again and press the spacebar.

This expands the Viewer workspace to full screen so that it is easier to see both Viewers.

6   Place your cursor over each Viewer and press Control-F to fit the Viewer to the image.

7   In one of the Viewers, toggle the Channel Viewer to the alpha channel, or you can just press A.

You can move a Viewer around by grabbing its title bar. You can also resize it by grabbing its borders. You can have as many Viewers as you want, and each is "live," assuming that the Update mode is not set to No Update (see the following section).

Viewer Update Modes

When you create a Viewer, it is assigned to the active node, so the Viewer will show something new every time you create a new node or click to evaluate a different node. To create a new Viewer window, choose Viewers > New Viewer.

> **NOTE** ▶ You can lock a Viewer to a node by double-clicking the Viewer and then clicking the node you want. Once you have assigned a Viewer to a specific node, you should create another Viewer to handle the duty of viewing the active node.

1   Adjust the Time Bar, and you can see that both Viewers update.

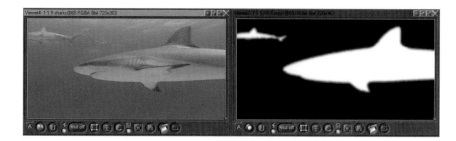

2   Try out the different Update modes in conjunction with adjusting the Time Bar. Click and hold the Update icon with the left mouse button and then select any of the three Viewer Update modes.

  ▶   Normal Update mode—Image is displayed when the frame render is finished.

▶   Scrolling Update mode—Image is presented as it is displayed, scrolling upward. Use this when you have large images and slow updates.

▶   No Update mode—No update until you toggle to Normal mode.

To kill the update of a Viewer, press the Esc key.

TIP ▶ The 3 key cycles the Update mode. Pressing 3 toggles forward and Shift-3 toggles backward. The cursor must be in the Viewer window.

3   Make sure the Update mode is returned to Normal.

4   Close the second Viewer that's showing the alpha channel, and move the remaining Viewer to the bottom-left corner of the screen.

5   Press the spacebar to return the Viewer workspace to normal size.

6   Place your cursor over the Viewer and press Shift-F to fit the Viewer to the desktop.

Now, you should be back to normal.

Comparing Images

If you want to compare two different images or two different planes within the same image, you can use the Compare buttons in the Viewer. In this example, you will compare the RGB planes with the alpha plane. The A and B tabs on the bottom left of the Viewer let you switch between two images.

1   Make sure the A tab is on top, and click the left side of the sharks node in
    the Node View.

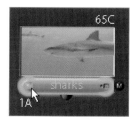

NOTE ▶ In case you were wondering, the 1A next to the node signifies
Viewer 1, Tab A.

This simply reloads the same image into the same Viewer and is therefore
redundant.

2   Click the A tab once to cycle it to the B tab.

3   Click the left side of the shark node again. This loads the same image into
    B tab.

4   With the cursor in the Viewer, press the A key, or toggle the Channel Viewer
    to the white dot icon to view the alpha channel.

5   You may have to click Home to center the image.

6   You can toggle between the A and B tabs to compare the images.

TIP ▶ The 1 key cycles the A and B tabs. Pressing 1 toggles forward and Shift-1 toggles backward. The cursor must be in the Viewer window.

7 If you click and hold the C at the bottom of the Viewer, the Compare mode button options pop up.

8 Select the Vertical Compare button.

9 Now grab the tiny little gray C icon in the lower-right corner of the Viewer and drag it left and right, revealing the two images.

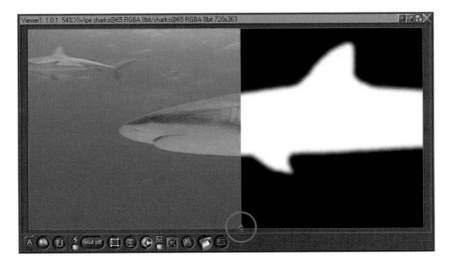

You can also use a horizontal or fading Compare mode.

TIP ▶ The 7 key cycles the Compare modes. Pressing 7 toggles forward, Shift-7 toggles backward. The cursor must be in the Viewer window.

10 Return Compare to Normal mode.

NOTE ▶ Make sure you turn off the Compare mode before continuing, because you may accidentally leave the mode looking entirely at the B image when you are working on the A image.

Creating Flipbooks to Play Back Clips

Can you just tell me how to play the darn clip already? All right, all right. To play the shark clip, you need to create a flipbook. A *flipbook* is a RAM-based image player that loads a clip into memory so it can be played back in real time. The first step is to set the frame range.

1 Click the Globals tab in the Parameters workspace.

This will load the Global parameters into the Parameters workspace.

2 Under timeRange, type *1-65* to load 65 frames.

1-65x2 means every other frame, 1-65x3 every third frame, and so on.

3 Now click the Flipbook icon at the bottom of the Viewer to launch a flip-book of your clip with the desired frame range.

TIP If you click and hold the right mouse button over the Flipbook icon, a Render Parameters page pops up, letting you specify your frame range and other settings. You can then set the frame range exactly as just described. Otherwise, it will use the Global settings you have specified.

4 You can press the right angle bracket (>) key at any time while the flip-book is loading to see the clip play. Shake will continue to render and add frames in the background.

If you press stop (the spacebar) before the flipbook is done loading, you can resume the load by pressing the slash (/) key. Given enough RAM, you can load as many flipbooks as you want.

5 Experiment with some of the flipbook shortcut keys listed at the end of this lesson.

6 When you are done playing around with the flipbook controls, close the flipbook by clicking the X in the top-left corner of the flipbook window.

Congratulations! You've made it through Lesson 1.

7 Exit Shake by choosing Shake > Quit Shake. Click No when prompted whether to save the script.

Lesson Review

1. What functions are contained in the Shake tool tabs?

2. How do you import images and sequences into Shake?

3. How do you compare two images or two different planes within an image in Shake?

4. How do you set your frame range and other settings for a flipbook?

5. What is the Viewer used for?

Answers

1. The tool tabs contain the various Shake processes that you can add to your process tree. Each node serves a particular function, such as color correction, image filtering, or layering. These nodes are logically placed in different tool tabs according to their functions.

2. You use the FileIn node to import images and sequences into Shake.

3. You can use the Compare buttons in the Viewer to compare different images, or different planes of one image. When you are done comparing images, make sure you return to Normal mode so that you don't accidentally leave the Viewer looking at the B image when you are working on the A buffer image.

4. Right-click the Flipbook icon to set the frame range and other settings for a flipbook.

5. You use the Viewer to play and view images.

Keyboard Shortcuts

Undo/Redo

Command-Z	undo
Command-Y	redo

> **NOTE ▶** Undo is disabled in the trial version of Shake that comes with this book's DVD.

Keyboard Shortcuts

General Windowing

Option–left mouse drag	pans window
middle mouse drag	pans window
spacebar	expands or collapses window
Control-Option-drag	zooms some windows in and out (Curve Editor, Node View, Time Bar)
Control–middle mouse drag	zooms some windows in and out (Curve Editor, Node View, Time Bar)
Esc	kills processing
U	updates Viewer
Shift–middle mouse drag on a tab	tears off a tab as a floating window (floating windows can be put back by simply closing them with the close button on the title bar)
Shift-Option–left mouse drag on a tab	tears off a tab as a floating window

Viewer

N	creates/copies new Viewer
Control-F	fits Viewer to image
Shift-F	fits Viewer to desktop
F	fits image to Viewer
Option-drag	pans image
Home	resets Viewer zoom and pan to default
R, G, B, A, C	toggles the red, green, blue, alpha, and RGB view planes
1	cycles the A and B tabs
2	cycles the R, G, B, A, and RGB channels

Keyboard Shortcuts

Viewer *(continued)*

3	cycles the Update modes
4	cycles the Viewer scripts
7	cycles the Compare modes
. (think of it as the > key)	plays forward
, (think of it as the < key)	plays backward

Flipbook

Shift-drag (in the flipbook windows)	scrubs clip
right arrow key	advances frames
left arrow key	steps back through frames
spacebar	stops/plays clip or render
/	continues loading/render
Home	recenters image
–/= (keys next to Delete)	zooms in and out
keypad + or –	increases or decreases the playback frame rate
T	real-time toggle; drops frames in playback
R, G, B, A, C	views red, green, blue, alpha, and color channels
H	in Compare mode, sets to horizontal split
V	in Compare mode, sets to vertical split
S	in Compare mode, switches split
F	in Compare mode, fades split
Esc	closes flipbook

2

Lesson 2
Basic Compositing

Digital compositing is the seamless integration of multiple elements—elements that may come from vastly different sources. A successful composite may rely on many techniques, such as keying/matting, color correcting, rotoscoping, and painting. At the end of the day, it's not what you did, but how the effect looks. Shake provides you with extensive tools to combine your elements into a seamless visual effect.

In this lesson you will composite four clips to create this scene.

Understanding Process Trees

Shake is composed of a collection of image manipulation engines—compositing, color correcting, warping, and so on. Each engine can be driven by a series of different commands, called *nodes*, or *processes*. These nodes are arranged into a treelike structure called a process tree. Shake saves a process tree into a file called a script. The terms *process tree* and *script* will be used interchangeably throughout this book. Nodes can be added or inserted at any time, building up an effect in a nonlinear fashion. It is a very flexible way to create an effect, and it's easy to change. So your clients can endlessly noodle with their shots, and you can make changes quickly thanks to Shake's flexibility.

Creating a Simple Tree

This section walks you through the process of creating a simple tree.

Loading Images

Before creating a process tree, you need to load in some images:

1   Open Shake.

2   Go to the Image tab and select the FileIn node.

    The File Browser will open up.

3   Navigate to the Lesson02 folder. You should see five sequences.

4   Click the Type heading to sort the clips by type.

5   Select the first file, **background.1-60#.iff**, and then click Next.

6   FileIn the remaining four sequences: **foreground.1-60#.iff**, **robot.1-60#.iff**, **robot_comp.1-60#.iff**, and **shadow.1-60#.iff**.

7   Close the File Browser when done.

> **TIP** ▶ You can select a file or sequence from the File Browser in one step by double-clicking it.

You now have five nodes in the Node View. They are background, foreground, robot, robot_comp, and shadow—all named automatically by Shake. Because the parameters of the last node you created pop into the Parameters workspace automatically, you can see the shadow parameters listed in the bottom-right window.

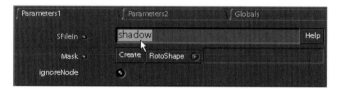

The first parameter shown is SFileIn, which should list shadow. If you want to rename the node, you can do so here. You can see the parameters of any node by clicking that node's right side, and you can view any node in the Viewer by clicking the node's left side.

8   If you want to see a fancy glow around your nodes, place your pointer over the Node View and press Control-E.

This is Enhanced Node View mode. When turned on, it draws a bluish glow around nodes that are animated. This includes nodes that are QuickTime movies or multiple-image sequences, nodes containing keyframed parameters, or nodes utilizing expressions that change a parameter's value over time.

NOTE ► Screen shots for this book were taken with Enhanced Node View on.

Click here to see an active node in the Viewer ——— robot_comp ——— Click here to see a node's parameters

If you double-click the node, you simultaneously load the node into the active Viewer and list its parameters in the Parameters workspace. If you drag the pointer over the nodes, you see the node name, function type, and image information in the contextual help field at the bottom center of the Shake screen.

robot_comp (SFileIn) 8bit RGBA 960x540

9 Click the left side of the robot_comp node to view the final shot.

You'll need to set the Globals timeRange parameter, but instead of typing it manually, you can use the Auto button to do it for you.

10 Go to the Globals tab in the Parameters workspace.

11 To the right of the timeRange parameter, click the Auto button.

timeRange   1-60   Auto

The Auto button sets the time range to the length of the longest FileIn node. In this case, the range is set to 1–60.

12 Click the Home icon at the bottom-right corner of the interface.

The Time Bar is automatically set to the Globals timeRange.

13 Now click the Flipbook icon at the bottom of the Viewer to launch a flipbook of your clip with the desired frame range.

14 Press the > key at any time while the clip is loading to see it play.

You can press the spacebar before the clip is done to stop loading it, and you can resume the load by pressing the spacebar again.

This is the final composite of the effect that you will be building.

The shot is a combination of four computer-generated elements. Your job will be to composite the elements together so that they look like one shot.

15 Close the flipbook.

> **NOTE ►** Whenever you are done playing a clip, close the flipbook window, because it eats up precious RAM when left open.

If you would like to see the finished commercial with music, you can view a QuickTime version of it, located in the Lesson02 folder.

16 Minimize Shake by double-clicking its title bar.

17 Navigate to your Lesson02 folder, double-click the **citroen_C4.mov** file, and play the clip.

This is really a fun commercial.

18 Close the QuickTime Player.

19 Maximize Shake by clicking its icon in the Dock.

Take a look at each of your elements.

20 Load the **background**, **foreground**, **robot**, and **shadow** clips into flipbooks and play them.

These are the elements you will be combining to create the composite. The foreground and background will be added together, then the shadow, and finally, the robot.

21 Close all open flipbooks.

22 Double-click the **robot** clip.

23 Toggle the Channel Viewer from full color to the white dot icon to view the alpha channel.

The **robot** clip has an alpha channel that you can use to place the robot over the background. Alpha channels are basically a cookie cutter, and they are the heart of compositing. It just goes to show how simple compositing is. In an alpha channel, the white areas represent your foreground, and black areas represent your background in the final composite. Because the **robot** clip is a computer-generated element, a single click of a button creates and embeds the alpha channel into the clip during the rendering process.

24 Place your pointer over the Viewer and press the C key to view the RGB channels.

Understanding Thumbnails

If you look at the Node workspace, you might notice the pretty thumbnails. Each of these is a function that you can look at and modify. It just so happens that these are all FileIn functions that read in images.

As you can see from the robot image above, the thumbnail also indicates transparency if there is an accompanying alpha channel.

A bit about the thumbnails:

▶   They use frame 1 as the thumbnail image by default.

▶   To refresh to the current frame, select the node and press R in the Node View.

▶ To see the alpha channel, place the pointer over the thumbnail and press A. To return to RGB color, press C with the pointer over the thumbnail.

▶ Any node can have a thumbnail—just select it and press T.

▶ To hide thumbnails, select the ones you want to hide and press T. Press T again to see the thumbnails.

▶ In the Globals tab, reveal the guiSettings to change the displayThumbnails control. This is the same as pressing T in the Node View.

Here's a nifty trick: Drag the robot node over the background node in the Node workspace.

Shake creates a minicomposite for you. Does this help you composite or change your tree at all? Not at all, but it's pretty cool, isn't it? To do an actual composite, you have to hook up the nodes. So just hold on, why don't ya?

Attaching Nodes

You can insert nodes into a tree in one of six ways:

▶ By choosing the node you want from the Tools menu at the top of the screen.

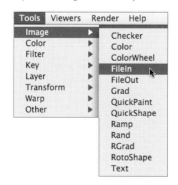

▶ By clicking one of the tool tab buttons in the bottom-left window of the Shake screen.

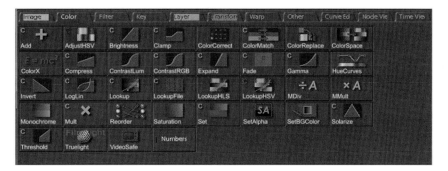

▶ By right-clicking any of the tool tab buttons in the bottom-left window of the Shake screen and choosing an insertion method.

▶ By right-clicking a tool tab and choosing a node from the pop-up menu.

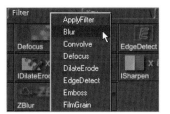

▶ By right-clicking the Node workspace and choosing from the Node menu.

▶ By copying and pasting an existing node. Command-C copies, Command-V pastes. You can also perform these functions by right-clicking in the Node workspace.

NOTE ► Copy and paste are disabled in the trial version of Shake that comes with this book.

To start compositing, you need to attach a Layer node. By default, nodes are attached to the active node. Now this is important, so pay attention: The active node is the one highlighted in green. You can highlight a clip by clicking it once.

1   Highlight the **foreground** clip by clicking it once, and select an Over function in the Layer tab.

The Over node attaches itself to the **foreground** clip automatically. Shake connects the output of the foreground to the left input of the Over1 node. The Over function places one image over another according to the matte of the foreground image.

2   Attach the **background** clip to the Over1 node. To do this, click the output knot (this is the small dot that appears at the bottom of the background node as you move your mouse over it) and drag to the right, or background, input of the Over1 node and release.

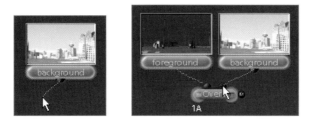

NOTE ► The standard practice for layering operations that involve two input images is to connect the foreground to the first (or left) input, and connect the background to the second (or right) input.

3   Place your pointer over the Viewer and press the F key so that you can see the entire image.

You should now see the background and foreground images composited as one. This composite will serve as the background for the robot.

The next step is to add the robot.

4   Highlight the **robot** clip and select another Over from the Layer tab.

5   Take the output of Over1 and connect it to the right input of Over2.

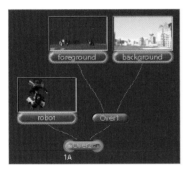

The color of the robot will need to be adjusted, but you'll do that in a moment.

Setting Resolution

You may have observed that the robot image has a lower resolution than the foreground and background images (960x540 pixels, compared with 1920x1080) and that the resolution of the composite is cropped to the larger size of the **foreground** and **background** clips. The resolution is displayed in the Viewer title bar, and in the help field at the bottom of the screen when you hover the pointer over a clip.

Shake allows you to composite images of different resolutions thanks to the clipMode parameter contained in every Layer node. In this case, the Over node defaults to the resolution of the **background** clip.

1   Toggle the clipMode back and forth to select the foreground or the background as your output resolution. When you're done, leave the clipMode set to foreground.

2   Place your pointer over the Viewer and press the F key to make the image larger.

At the lower resolution, the background is clipped to its lower-left corner and would look a lot better if it were resized to fit the resolution of the **robot** clip.

3   Highlight Over1 and select a Resize node from the Transform tab.

4   Double-click the 1920 number field, type *960,* and press Return.

5   Double-click the 1080 number field, type *540,* and press Return.

The new size looks much better.

Premultiplication

For the Over node, the most frequently used Layer node, Shake assumes there is an alpha channel to determine the foreground pixels, and that the foreground image is premultiplied by that mask. Most computer-generated elements are premultiplied. This includes the robot element.

Let me define a *premultiplied* image: It is an image that has its RGB channels multiplied by its alpha channel. Typically, images rendered by 3D software are premultiplied, meaning the transparent areas have black both in the RGB areas and in the same areas of the alpha channel. In a premultiplied image, the value of the RGB channels is never higher than that of the alpha channel.

Scanned elements or other 2D-generated plates require an added alpha channel (also called the matte or mask channel), which is then used to premultiply that image with an optional setting in the Over node. To get that alpha channel, draw it with Shake's QuickPaint or RotoShape node or pull a key with Shake's keying functions. If the alpha channel is provided to you, read it in and then copy it into a foreground image's alpha channel with a SwitchMatte node. Once you premultiply, you can composite. For a more detailed explanation on premultiplication, refer to the Shake documentation.

Saving Your Tree

Before continuing, you should save your tree. Shake saves the tree as a script. A script is a text file that contains all of the information about your tree. The script can be loaded back into Shake for later work and can be rendered either from within the software or from the command line.

TIP ▸ To make your life easier, I have included a completed script not only for this lesson, but for all of them. If you ever get stuck, you can view the finished script in each lesson's folder by using File > Open Script.

NOTE ▸ Skip this exercise if you are using the trial version of Shake.

To Save your tree:

1   Select File > Save Script.

2   Create a new folder in your own home directory to save your scripts and images: Navigate to your home directory, and click the Create New Folder icon at the top right of the File Browser.

3   When prompted, type *Shake_Output* for the name of the folder, and then click OK.

4   Type *robot_pt1* for the name of your script and click OK.

Shake automatically adds a .shk extension to the end of your filename when it saves.

NOTE ▶ If you forget to save the script and exit Shake, you could select File > Recover Script to recall the last autosaved version.

Inserting, Replacing, and Creating Nodes

When you click a tool in the tool tabs, that tool is inserted after the currently selected node (highlighted in green).

1   Click the robot node so that it turns green, and from the Color tab, select Brightness.

A Brightness1 node is inserted between the robot node and the Over2 node.

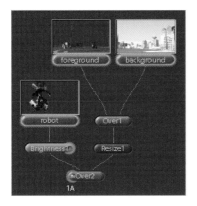

Right-clicking any function in the tool tabs will give you five different insertion choices for that particular node: Insert, Branch, Replace, Create, and Insert Multiple.

2 Right-click the Gamma function in the Color tab and choose Branch.

A new branch of the tree is created for the Gamma1 node off the Brightness1 node.

3   Right-click the Compress function in the Color tab and choose Replace.

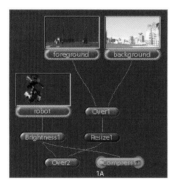

The Gamma1 node is replaced by the Compress1 node.

4   Right-click Add in the Color tab and choose Create.

A new, unconnected Add1 node is added to the Node workspace.

5   Drag the Add1 node directly over the connecting line between robot and Brightness1 so that both its knots appear highlighted. You can select which input of a multi-input node to insert by dragging the node to the left or right to highlight the desired input knot.

6   When you release the mouse button, the node is inserted automatically.

You may have noticed when right-clicking a node in the tool tabs that each node insertion option has associated keyboard shortcuts. The keyboard shortcuts are listed at the end of this lesson for your reference.

Selecting Nodes

There are various ways to select and deselect nodes. Here are some of them:

► Drag over the robot, Add1, and Brightness1 nodes to select them. If you drag a selection box over any node in the Node View, the node will be selected.

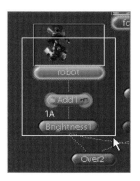

► Control-drag over the robot and Add1 nodes to deselect them. If you Control-drag over previously selected nodes in the Node View, you deselect them.

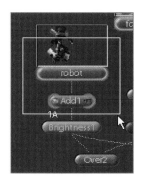

▶   Press Command-A to select all nodes.

▶   Click the background area to deselect all nodes.

If you right-click in the Node workspace, you'll see quite a few other tree selection options along with their keyboard shortcuts.

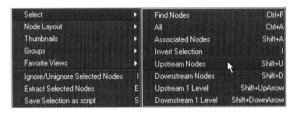

Detaching and Deleting Nodes

To delete a connection, position the pointer over the connecting line until it turns red or yellow, and press Delete on your keyboard. (On Macintosh laptops, press fn-Delete.)

1   Place the pointer over the connecting line between Brightness1 and Compress1, and press the Delete key. Alternatively, click a node and drag violently back and forth, like a squirrel shaking a nut, until the node separates.

To delete nodes, select them and press the Delete key.

2   Click the Compress1 node and press the Delete key.

3   Click the Brightness1 node and press the Delete key.

Organizing Nodes

For those of you who like to keep your Node workspace as tidy as your closets, Shake provides several node-organization features:

▶ Grab active nodes to drag them around.

▶ To organize all nodes, deselect them all and press L, for layout.

▶ To organize specific nodes, select the nodes and press L.

Editing Parameters

Before continuing, make sure your tree looks like the following image:

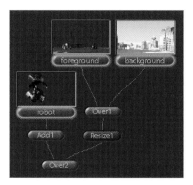

The composite is almost done, but the color of the robot is not quite matched. The Add function, which adds color to the R, G, and B channels, is going to take care of this for you. It's a nifty way to modify the color of an image.

1   Click the left side of the Over2 node to see it in the Viewer.

2 Click the right side of the Add1 node to see its parameters in the Parameters workspace.

This configuration will let you view one node while editing the parameters of another. Without the capability to separately view and edit nodes, it would be like blowing down a West Texas country road at midnight. That's bad, real bad. The Add1 node has red, green, blue, and alpha channel parameters.

3 Click the plus sign (+) to the left of the Color parameter.

A + next to a parameter means that more parameters can be revealed.

In this case, a series of radio buttons is revealed.

4 Click the + next to the R radio button.

The opening of nested parameters reminds me of one of those annoying gifts where smaller and smaller boxes are inside each other.

5   Click the number field for Red, type *.20*, and press Return.

What the #$%? The whole image brightened up, not just the robot. That's because you have just broken a most important rule: Don't color-correct a premultiplied image. If you do, you may have problems with edges or with unwanted changes to global levels. Many people see this type of error and assume it is a mask problem, so they make the mask smaller in an attempt to get rid of the edge. Heathens! Happily, these problems are easily solved through the proper handling of premultiplied images.

To solve this problem, you must first add an MDiv (matte divide) node from the Color tab to divide the robot's RGB channels by its alpha channel. This undoes the premultiplication. Second, you must activate the preMultiply parameter in the Over node. Then you can color-correct to your heart's content.

6   Highlight the robot node and select an MDiv node from the Color tab.

7   Click the right side of the Over2 node to edit its parameters and activate preMultiply.

Now, only the robot is color-corrected.

8 Click the right side of the Add1 node and reopen the Color submenus by repeating steps 3 and 4.

When you entered .20 in the Red parameter, the Green and Blue values were automatically set to the same value. Shake does some parameter linking for you within various nodes; this is signified by the + next to a parameter.

9 Click the + next to Green.

It says Red, which means that the Green parameter is linked to Red. Whenever Red is adjusted, Green will be set to the same value. If you don't want the parameters to be linked, you can type a new value in the number field or drag the slider of the linked parameter.

10 In the number fields for Green and Blue, type *0* and press Return.

But wait, there's more. Instead of typing a value into a field, we can do a little drag and drop: You can drag from one parameter to another and transfer values.

11 Enter *0.03* in the Red field.

12 Click the Red parameter name, drag, and release on the Blue parameter name.

When you click the Red parameter name, a mutant three-fingered hand appears. It disappears when you release the mouse button over the Blue parameter name. The value from Red is transferred to the Blue parameter.

You can also create a link from one parameter to another by pressing Shift when you drag and drop.

13 Set the Blue parameter to *–0.03*.

14 Shift-click the Blue parameter name and drag onto the Green parameter name.

A + appears to the left of the Green parameter.

15 Click the + next to the Green parameter.

The expression bar appears, with NRiScript1.Add1.blue listed as an expression for the Green parameter. This is called *parameter linking* and can be done not only within a node, but also between other nodes in your tree. Parameter linking is covered in more detail in Lesson 12.

16 To remove this expression, click the number field for Green, type *0*, and press Return.

To see the effect of the Add color correction, use the I (ignore) keyboard shortcut.

17 Click Add1 to make it the active node.

18 With the pointer over the Node view, press the I key.

Observe how the correction changes the robot in the Viewer. It has a slight warming effect.

Creating a Drop Shadow

To make the robot really fit into the scene, it needs a drop shadow. You will make one by using a Brightness node to darken the background but limit the adjustment only to the area of a supplied shadow mask.

1 Insert a Brightness node from the Color tab between the Resize1 and Over2 nodes.

Do I really need to explain what the Brightness node does? I sure hope not.

2 Drag a connecting line from the output of the **shadow** clip to the right side of the Brightness1 node.

An M appears on the side of the node. This is the Mask input.

3 In the Brightness1 node, click the + to the left of the Mask control to
expand the Mask parameters.

You can apply a mask to any operation by dragging the output of a node
to the right side of a second node. That node will process only within the
white areas of the channel you specify. When a node has a mask applied to
it, new parameters will appear in the Parameters workspace, letting you
activate the mask, invert the mask, and control the mask's strength.

The other way to apply a mask to a node is through the Mask Create
function. When you click the RotoShape pop-up menu next to the Mask
Create button, you can choose from six mask-creation options that will
automatically create a node and connect it to the Mask input of the node
you are editing.

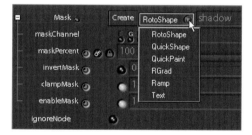

Because the maskChannel parameter is set to use the alpha channel by
default, and the **shadow** clip has values only in the RGB channels, you'll
need to select a different channel.

4   Click G for the maskChannel parameter.

The Brightness1 node will use this channel when creating the drop shadow.

5   Set the Brightness1 Value parameter to *0.25*.

The entire screen darkens except for the shadow area because, by default, the mask settings process only within the white areas of the channel you specify. The mask should be reversed.

6   Activate invertMask.

The shadow now looks correct.

Rendering Your Tree

The final step is to save your script and render the darn thing.

1   Select the node you want to actually render, in this case the Over2 node.

2   Select FileOut in the Image tab.

3   Navigate to your home directory and select the Shake_Output folder that you created earlier in this lesson.

NOTE ▶ If you are using the trial version of Shake and skipped the saving exercise earlier in this lesson, perform steps 2 and 3 on page 54.

4   Enter the filename *my_robot_comp.#.iff* at the bottom of the File Browser
and click OK.

The image filename should contain three components:

▶   A description of the image.

▶   A symbol for the frame, either # or @, to represent a padded or
unpadded placeholder. Padded frame numbers include leading zeros
before the actual frame number. For instance, frame 1 of a four-digit
padded number would look like **test.0001.iff**. Frame one of an unpadded
number would look like **test.1.iff**.

▶   An extension: *.iff* for an IFF file, *.tif* for a TIFF file, *.tga* for a TGA file,
and so on. There are about 20 different formats, which can be viewed in a
FileOut's fileFormat pull-down.

NOTE ▶   The IFF file format is Shake's native file format.

Therefore, if you enter a name such as *test.#.iff*, Shake will write out
test.0001.iff, test.0002.iff, and so on. If you type *test.@.cin*, your output
files will write out as test.1.cin, test.2.cin, test.3.cin, and so on.

5   If you are using the full version of Shake, resave the tree by choosing
File > Save Script.

NOTE ▶   The saving of scripts is disabled in the trial version of Shake.

6   Right-click the my_robot_comp node and choose Render > Render
FileOut Nodes from the pop-up menu.

The Render Parameters window will appear.

7   The default settings are fine, so just click Render.

A Monitor window will show you the progress of your render. Unlike a normal flipbook, only the current frame is loaded into memory. Previous frames are discarded from the Monitor window. Additionally, the Monitor window is always the same resolution (360x240), regardless of the output resolution settings. When the render finishes, you can load the frames into a flipbook to see them.

8   When the render is finished, close the Monitor window.

9   Open up a new FileIn node, and if you don't see the file you just rendered, click the Force Update button at the top right of the File Browser.

This refreshes the File Browser, and you should see your rendered sequence listed.

10   Double-click the **my_robot_comp.1-60#.iff** sequence you just rendered.

11 Click the Flipbook icon to load `my_robot_comp`.

12 Press the > key to play the clip.

Pat yourself on the back; you've created and rendered your first Shake composite.

13 Quit Shake.

Lesson Review

1. How do you attach nodes in the Node workspace?

2. What is the connection order of node inputs?

3. What is the keyboard shortcut that organizes the Node workspace?

4. Does the Over node expect premultiplied or non-premultiplied images?

5. What node undoes premultiplication?

6. How do you create a node thumbnail?

7. What is the method for applying a mask to a node?

Answers

1. You can attach nodes in the Node workspace by clicking on one of the tool tab buttons, right-clicking any of the tool tab buttons, or using the Tools menu.

2. The standard practice for layering operations that involve two input images is to connect the foreground to the first (or left) input, and connect the background to the second (or right) input.

3. You can automatically organize your nodes by deselecting them all and pressing the L key.

4. The Over node expects premultiplied images.

5. The MDiv (matte divide) node undoes premultiplication.

6. Any node can have a thumbnail—just select it and press T.

7. You can apply a mask to any operation by dragging the output of a node to the right side of a second node.

Keyboard Shortcuts

TOOL TABS

Left-click	inserts a node after the selected node
Shift-click	creates new branch off the selected node
Control-click	replaces the currently selected node
Shift-Control-click	creates an unconnected node

NODE WORKSPACE

O	toggles on the Overview window to help navigate in the Node View
Control-E	activates enhanced Node View
I	turns off selected nodes when activated; select them again and press I to reactivate

Keyboard Shortcuts

NODE WORKSPACE *(continued)*

E	pulls the active nodes from the tree, reconnecting the remaining nodes to each other
S	saves a selection as a script

Edit

Command-X	removes selected nodes and places them into the paste buffer
Command-C	copies the selected nodes into the paste buffer
Command-V	pastes nodes and text into the Node View
Shift-Command-V	pastes linked nodes
Delete	deletes the selected nodes
fn-Delete	deletes the selected nodes on a Macintosh laptop
Command-Z	undoes up to 100 steps
Command-Y	redoes your steps unless you have changed values after several undos

View

+	zooms in to the Node View
–	zooms out of the Node View
Home	centers all nodes
F	frames all selected nodes into the Node View

Keyboard Shortcuts

NODE WORKSPACE *(continued)*

Select

Command-F	activates nodes according to what to you enter in the Search string field
Command-A	selects all nodes
Shift-A	selects all nodes attached to the current group
!	inverts the selection
Shift-U	selects nodes upstream from the currently active node
Shift-D	selects nodes downstream from the currently active node
Shift–up arrow	adds one upstream node to the current selection
Shift–down arrow	adds one downstream node to the current selection

Node Layout

L	performs an automated layout on the selected nodes
X	snaps all selected nodes into the same column
Y	snaps all selected nodes into the same row

Thumbnails

R	refreshes the thumbnail at the current frame
T	hides/shows thumbnails
A	shows the alpha channel of thumbnail
C	displays thumbnails in full color

Keyboard Shortcuts

NODE WORKSPACE *(continued)*

Groups

G	visually collapses selected nodes into one node; press again to ungroup
Alt-G	groups selected nodes and maximizes them
Shift-G	consolidates selected groups
Control-G	ungroups selected nodes/groups

Macros

Shift-M	launches the MacroMaker with the selected nodes as the macro body
B	opens up a macro into a subwindow so you can review wiring and parameters
Alt-B	closes up the macro subwindow when the pointer is placed outside the open macro

PARAMETERS WORKSPACE

Control-drag (while over a parameter value)	changes the value interactively; left-drag to lower the value, right-drag to raise the value
Tab	advances to the next text field
Shift-Tab	goes to the previous text field
right-click	accesses a pop-up menu
drag a parameter name	copies a parameter to the target parameter
Shift-drag a parameter name	links a parameter from the target parameter

3

Lesson Files	APTS_Shake > Lessons > Lesson03
Media	robot_pt1.shk
	lights.1-60#.iff
	robot_final.1-60#.iff
Time	This lesson takes approximately 1 hour to complete.
Goals	Make a drop shadow from scratch
	Create and edit keyframes to animate over time
	Create a vignette, or soft fade
	Add realistic glows and match film grain

Intermediate Compositing

Normally you can get 95 percent of a shot done very quickly. It's always that last 5 percent that takes the majority of the time and effort but makes the difference in whether the shot looks real. In this lesson, which continues the robot composite, you will use keyframing to animate parameters as well as use masks to limit the effect of filters.

You can see the motion path in Shake as you set keyframes.

From Robot to Robzilla

Before we start this lesson, let's have a little fun. It's interesting how our mind can perceive an object totally differently based on perspective. You'll see what I mean in a moment.

1   Open Shake.

2   Choose File > Open Script.

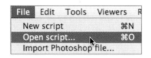

3   Navigate to the Lesson02 folder and choose **robot_pt1.shk**, or select the script that you saved from the previous lesson, and click OK.

Your script opens up in the Node workspace.

4   Highlight the Brightness1 node and press I to ignore it.

5   Select the Add1 node and choose Outside from the Layer tab.

Outside places an image outside the mask of a second image. Only the mask of the second image is considered in the composite, and the color comes from the foreground image. Essentially, the mask of the second image cuts a hole in the first image.

6   Connect Resize1 to the right input of Outside1.

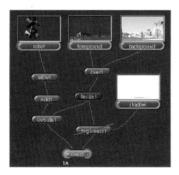

7 Double-click the Over2 node and click the Flipbook icon.

Holy Toledo! The robot looks gigantic! The cute little robot has turned into a scary Robzilla.

| Robot | Robzilla |

OK, quit messing around.

Creating a Drop Shadow from Scratch

In Lesson 2, you created a drop shadow using a premade computer-generated shadow element. This is ideal, but oftentimes you have to improvise and make your own shadow.

1 Choose File > Reload Script and click Yes when asked whether you want to reload the script and lose the most recent changes.

2 Highlight the **shadow** clip and delete it.

3 Select the **robot** clip and Shift-click a Move2D node on the Transform tool tab to create a branch.

The Move2D function combines many of the other transform nodes, including Pan, Scale, Shear, and Rotate.

4   Connect the output of Move2D1 to the mask input of Brightness1.

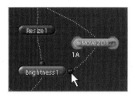

5   Look at the alpha channel in the Viewer.

The Brightness1 node will use this alpha channel when creating the drop shadow.

6   Change the Viewer so you can see the RGB channels.

7   Double-click the Brightness1 node and click the plus sign (+) to the left of the Mask control to expand the Mask parameters.

8   Deactivate invertMask and set the maskChannel to A for alpha.

The image in the area of the robot's alpha channel darkens and is ready to be positioned.

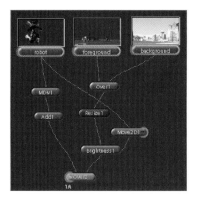

9   View the Over2 node and edit the Move2D1 node.

When the parameters for Move2D1 appear, Shake conveniently pops up some onscreen controls in the Viewer to help you.

The button that turns on the onscreen controls is located under the Viewer and has three positions.

10   Click and hold the onscreen controls button to see the options.

▶ This means the controls are always on. This is the mode you want to be in to interactively drag an image around.

▶ The controls disappear if you move the image. They reappear when you release the mouse button.

▶ The controls are always off, but you can still move the image in the Viewer by using the sliders in the Parameters workspace.

The onscreen controls work as shown here:

Move center of rotation and scale (holding down Control or Command)

Constrain pan vertically or horizontally (drag anywhere for free-form panning)

Scale horizontally   Scale uniformly   Scale vertically   Rotate

If you don't like the colors of the onscreen controls, you can change them by clicking the onscreen controls color swatch, which gives you access to the Color Picker.

11 Click the onscreen controls color swatch to open the Color Picker in the Node workspace.

12 In the Palette, click the red color square.

The onscreen controls turn red.

13 Click the white square to turn the onscreen controls back to white.

Now that you know how to turn the onscreen controls on and off and change their colors, you can be trusted to use the Move2D node. Just don't smash anything.

14 Click the Node View tab in the Node workspace to close the Color Picker and see your nodes.

15 Play around with the various onscreen controls to position the shadow.

When you use the onscreen controls, you are automatically entering values for the xPan, yPan, angle, xScale, and yScale parameters in the Move2D node. You can also adjust these parameters by moving the sliders.

TIP A cool trick is to Control-drag in the numeric text field on the slider. This gives you virtual sliders with finer control that go beyond the range of the graphic sliders.

Before you proceed, you should reset the node. This will bring all of the parameters back to their default settings.

16 Reset the Move2D1 parameters by right-clicking in the Parameters1 window and choosing Reset All Values.

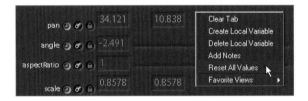

17 Use the onscreen controls to move the shadow down a bit so that you can see it.

18 Set the scale to *1.9* and *0.035*.

19 Drag in the image area to move the shadow under the robot's feet. I set my Pan parameters to 389.9 and –243.0.

20 Turn off the onscreen controls for a moment to get a better look at the shadow.

The shadow needs just a wee bit of softness.

21 Insert a Blur node from the Filter tab between the Move2D1 node and the Brightness1 node.

22 Set the first pixels field to 6.

Did you notice that the second pixels field value was set automatically? Shake is always making life easier for you.

23 Drag the Time Bar to view the composite and end on frame 60.

The shadow is no longer aligned under the robot's feet.

Animating over Time

To fix the position of the shadow, you need to animate it over time. Animation is the process of setting values at various frames, or *keyframes,* as they are called. These keyframes transition from one to another over time.

1 Move the Time Bar to frame 1.

2 Click the right side of Move2D1 to edit its parameters.

3 Turn the onscreen controls to the position at which they disappear when moving but reappear when you release the mouse.

4 If the AutoKey button under the Viewer is not highlighted green, click it to turn it on.

By turning on the Viewer's AutoKey button, you can enter keyframes using the onscreen controls. The AutoKey button under the Viewer is available for any node that has onscreen controls.

5 Position the shadow to your liking with the onscreen controls.

6 Go to frame 30 and position the shadow.

There are now little notches in the Time Bar where you have set keyframes at frames 1 and 30.

If you position the Time Bar over one of the notches, you can delete that keyframe by clicking the Delete Keyframe button in the Viewer.

7 Place the Time Bar at frame 30, and click the Delete Keyframe button in the Viewer.

If you turn off the AutoKey button and reposition the shadow, your changes will be ignored as soon as you move to a different frame. You can also add keys to a specific parameter by going to that parameter's slider and turning on its specific AutoKey button.

NOTE ▶ When the Viewer's AutoKey button is activated and you're using the onscreen controls, keyframes are set for all parameters. This is true even if you adjust only one parameter, such as rotation. Turning on the AutoKey button next to a particular parameter will set keyframes for that parameter only.

8 Go to frame 20 and turn on the AutoKey button next to the pan parameters.

Whenever you enter a value either with the sliders or the virtual sliders, that value will be entered as a keyframe.

NOTE ▶ You can't set keyframes with the parameter sliders by turning on the AutoKey button under the Viewer. To set keyframes with the sliders, you must turn on the AutoKey button next to the parameter.

9   Go to frame 40 and use the virtual sliders (Control-drag) in the Pan fields to position the shadow.

TIP ▶ If you want to enter a key but don't want to leave the AutoKey on, simply double-click the AutoKey button when it is off and a keyframe will be entered.

10 Position the shadow on frame 60.

You may have noticed that a motion path has been drawn on the screen as you have been setting keyframes. If you can't see the motion path, move your pointer over the Viewer area.

The display of the motion path is controlled by the Point display pop-up.

11 Click and hold the Point icon to see the pop-up list.

▶ Display motion path spline and keys

▶ Display motion path keys only

▶ Display neither motion path nor keys

You can drag points on the motion path and modify them. When you hover over or grab a point, the *x-y* coordinate is displayed, along with the frame number. You may need to zoom in on the points of the motion path to see this information.

12 If you had difficulty in positioning the shadow to match, use the following table to see the keyframes that I used for the completed shot:

Frame	xPan	yPan
1	389.9	−243.0
20	405.4	−232.5
40	422.3	−224.9
60	331.1	−232.1

13 Navigate to the new keyframes that have been set using the step forward/backward keyframe buttons at the bottom right of the screen.

14 Make a flipbook to see what you've done so far.

Not bad, but you can make it even better.

15 Close the flipbook.

Applying the Finishing Touches

The robot composite is almost finished, and it looks pretty good. It just needs a few finishing touches. It would look better if we added the following effects: brighter headlights, glowing highlights, a dark vignette, and film grain.

Color-Correcting the Headlights

The headlights of the car are a tad dim and definitely could be brightened up.

1 FileIn the `lights.1-60#.iff` clip from the Lesson03 folder.

2 Drag through the Time Bar to see the lights image.

This lights image will be used to isolate and color-correct only the headlights. 3D artists like to render separate elements in the form of mattes so that you, the 2D artist, have ultimate flexibility when putting all the pieces together.

3 Highlight Add1 and insert a Brightness node from the Color tab.

4   Connect the output of the lights node to the Mask input of Brightness2.

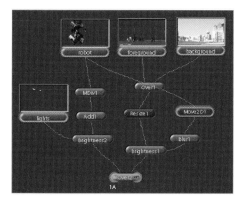

5   Open the Mask Parameters and choose G for the maskChannel.

Because the alpha channel for the lights image has a different shape from that of the headlights, we can use the green channel instead.

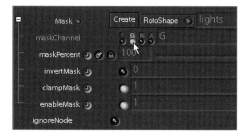

6   Click the left side of the Over2 node so that you can see what you are doing.

7   Set the Value parameter to *1.8*.

Woof! Now, you say, why woof? *Woof* is a technical term used when a setting has hit its perfect mark. I used to work as cameraman back in the day, and in the course of making equipment adjustments, engineers barked out a "woof," indicating that it was time to stop. You should stop adjusting at 1.8 because it is a good setting, so as I said, woof!

Adding a Glow

Adding a glow to the highlights is a great way to spice up the image and give it a more filmlike quality. Using a LumaKey, blurring the result, and adding it back to the original image can create a simple glow.

1 Select the robot node and Shift-click LumaKey on the Key tab.

Shift-clicking creates a new branch.

LumaKey creates a key in the alpha channel based on overall luminance. Values below loVal are set to black, and those above hiVal are set to white.

2 Activate the matteMult parameter and set loVal to *0.35* and hiVal to *0.65.*

The resulting image is a representation of the image's highlights.

3 Click Blur from the Filter tab.

4 Set the Pixels parameter to *140.*

Blurring the LumaKey prior to adding it to the original image generates the glow effect.

5 Add an IAdd function from the Layer tab after Over2, and connect Blur2 into the right input.

IAdd is a function that adds one image to another.

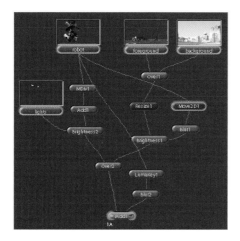

6   Set the Percent parameter to *60*.

Glow is natural, glow is good. Not everybody does it, but everybody should. Glow is natural, glow is fun. Glow is best when it's … one on one. OK, OK, I'll stop.

Creating a Vignette

A *vignette*, or soft fade, is a popular photographic effect in which the photo gradually darkens around the edges, usually in an oval shape. Wouldn't you say that the robot is just begging for a vignette? Well, I would.

1   Add a Brightness node from the Color tab after IAdd1.

2   Set the Value to *0.3*.

This darkens the entire image. What we really want is to darken only the edges of the screen. This can be accomplished by using an RGrad, which generates a radial gradation.

RGrad is located on the Image tab, but within all nodes you can create an RGrad that will be connected to the Mask input automatically.

3   Choose RGrad from the RotoShape pop-up menu next to the Mask Create setting.

I know, I know. The image is getting dark in the center of the gradation, so it will need to be inverted.

4   Click the right side of the Brightness3 node to edit its parameters.

5 Open the Mask parameters and activate invertMask.

6 Set the Res parameters for RGrad1 to *960* and *540* to match the resolution of the composite.

7 Set the aspectRatio, radius, falloffRadius, and falloff to create a darkened border around the edges of the screen.

Here are the values I used:

Parameter	Value
aspectRatio	1.3
radius	266
falloffRadius	419
falloff	0.8

Don't freak out, you're almost done.

Simulating Film Grain

To finish off the composite, the robot needs to have grain added so that it matches the grain of the **background** clip. The FilmGrain node is used to simulate film grain and is especially useful for adding grain to computer-generated elements. You may apply grain from a preset film stock, match grain to an existing plate, or set your own grain by adjusting sliders. In this exercise, you will match the grain of the **background** clip to the robot.

1   Place a FilmGrain node from the Filter tab after Brightness3.

The grain is everywhere, but you want it to appear only on the robot. The FilmGrain's Mask input can take care of this.

2   Connect an output of the robot node to the Mask input of the FilmGrain1 node.

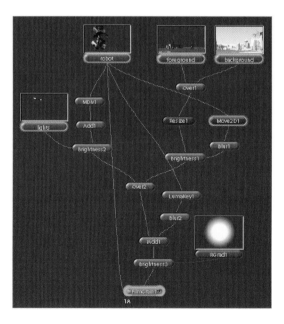

The grain becomes limited to the area within the robot mask. The next step is to place a sample box in an area of the background from which you want to sample the grain. The area should be very flat without detail, otherwise, the grain analysis may be inaccurate. Small elements will be perceived as grain detail, so the best area in the **background** clip would be the sky to the right of the robot.

3   Click the sky to the right of the robot to add a sample box.

You can add as many sample boxes as you want, but for this exercise you are drawing only one.

NOTE ▶ If you want to remove the grain sample box, click the Undo Last Region icon (left). Click the Reset the Regions icon (right) to remove all boxes and start over.

4   Now that you have the grain sample box in place, click the Analyze the Grain icon in the Viewer.

This sets the parameters in the FilmGrain node to match the grain of the **background** clip, and it does a pretty good job.

But hold on a minute. The grain is too heavy in the shadow areas. To fix this, you can adjust the filmResponse parameters to a higher value, which will cause the grain to be more apparent in the brighter areas of the robot.

5   Click the + next to filmResponse to expand its parameters.

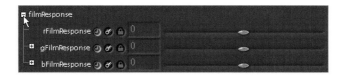

6   Set rFilmResponse to 0.5 and the grain will be less apparent in the shadow areas.

For those of you interested in minutiae, the FilmGrain node has the following parameters:

Parameter	Function
intensity	sets the intensity of the grain
grainSize	sets the size of the grain
aspectRatio	sets the aspect ratio of the grain to compensate for anamorphic or nonsquare pixel distortion
seed	sets the random seed for the grain
filmStock	allows the user to select from preset film stocks
r, g, b StdDev	this value is multiplied by the amount parameter; a higher value indicates more variation in the grain, making it more apparent
r, g, b Softness	controls the softness of the grain
r, g, b FilmResponse	determines the distribution of the grain relative to the luminance of the image; for grain to appear more in the white areas, push the value toward 1
colorCorr	specifies the apparent color saturation of the grain

The composite looks good, so it's time to make a flipbook—but not just any flipbook. Imagine being able to render a flipbook as a QuickTime movie, play it, and save it if you like it. Well, on Mac OS X, you can render to a temporary QuickTime file. This allows you to play extremely long clips. Once the flipbook is rendered, you can then save it using QuickTime's built-in features.

7 Right-click the FilmGrain1 node and choose Render > Render Disk FlipBook.

Render	▶	Render Flipbook...
Overview	O	Render Disk FlipBook...
Enhanced Node View	Ctrl+E	Render FileOut Nodes...
Snap to Grid		Render Cache Nodes...
Select	▶	Render Proxies...

8 In the Render Parameters window, click Render.

Shake pre-renders the QuickTime movie.

Pre-Rendering...

Once pre-rendered, the QuickTime movie is ready to play.

9   Click the Play button at the bottom left of the Shake Preview window to
    watch the QuickTime movie.

    If you'd like, you can save the QuickTime movie from the Shake
    QuickTime Viewer's File menu.

10 Quit the Shake QuickTime Viewer.

11 To compare your render with the final comp, you can create a flipbook of
    the **robot_final.1-60#.iff** clip, located in the Lesson03 folder.

    That's it. You can go home now.

12 Quit Shake.

Lesson Review

1.   How do you mask an operation?

2.   Define animation.

3.   What is a vignette?

4.   Describe some of the capabilities of the FilmGrain node.

5.   What is the technical term that indicates that a setting has reached its
     perfect mark?

Answers

1.   You can apply a mask to any operation by dragging the output of a node
     to the right side of a second node. That node will process only within the
     white areas of the channel you specify.

2.   Animation is the process of setting values at various frames, or *keyframes*.

3. A *vignette*, or soft fade, is a popular photographic effect in which the photo gradually darkens around the edges, usually in an oval shape.

4. With the FilmGrain node, you may apply grain from a preset film stock, match grain to an existing plate, or set your own grain by adjusting sliders.

5. Woof!

4

Lesson Files	APTS_Shake > Lessons > Lesson04
Media	woman.1-70.iff
	laser.1-70.iff
	woman_roto.shk
Time	This lesson takes approximately 2 hours to complete.
Goals	Draw and animate spline-based shapes
	Navigate the various functions of the RotoShape node
	Create multiple rotoshapes for a walking person
	Use the MultiLayer node to combine multiple shapes
	Add motion blur to create photorealistic shape animations

RotoShape

A rotoscope is a mechanical device that was patented by Max Fleischer in 1917. It projected single frames of live-action footage onto an animator's drawing board. By simply tracing the projected shape, the animator could quickly produce incredibly lifelike drawings. With the passage of time, *rotoscoping* (or "roto" for short) has become a generic term for manually extracting, isolating, or affecting a portion of an image. It is tedious work, but it's one of the most important parts of the visual effects process.

Shapes are often created on a frame-by-frame basis to extract or isolate a portion of the image. Shake's RotoShape node can create multiple spline-based shapes that can then be fed in as an alpha channel for an element, or used to mask a layer or an effect.

RotoShape has many convenient features:

▶ You can create multiple shapes within the same node.

▶ You can have a soft-edge falloff that can be modified on a knot-by-knot basis for each shape.

▶ You can make one shape cut a hole into another.

▶ When you break tangents, they remain at the angle at which you leave them until you modify them again.

NOTE ▶ In Shake 4.0 the black holes feature does not punch a hole in a rotoshape's alpha mask. Therefore, if you are using this as a mask, either use one of the RGB channels as the mask or reorder the luminance into the alpha when you use it with Inside or Outside. You can do this with Reorder–rgbl or a LumaKey at the default settings.

Add Shapes vs. Edit Shapes

1 Open Shake.

2 On the Image tab, select the RotoShape node.

When the RotoShape node is active, the associated tools appear on the Viewer toolbar.

There are two modes in RotoShape: Add Shapes mode (below, left) and Edit Shapes mode (below, right). You draw your initial shape and add shapes in the Add Shapes mode, and you modify or animate the shape in Edit Shapes mode.

3 Start by clicking a blank spot in the Viewer.

When you click a blank spot, a new knot (or point) appears there. As you click, if you drag away from the knot, tangents are created.

4 Continue the shape by dragging away from the knots as you draw to create tangents.

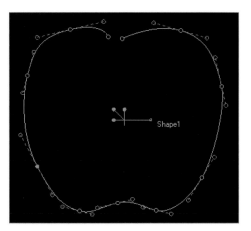

In Add Shapes mode, the shape does not render until you close the shape.

5 To close the shape, click the first knot that you added to the Viewer.

When you are in Add Shapes mode, the shape will not draw (and will therefore not affect later nodes). When you close the shape by clicking the first knot, Shake automatically switches you to Edit Shapes mode. In this mode, if you click a blank spot and drag, you are now selecting knots.

Either drag to select a new group of knots, Shift-drag to add to your group of active knots, or Command-drag to remove from your active group of knots.

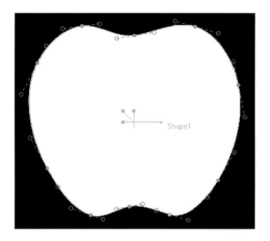

Inserting and Modifying Points and Tangents

1   Insert a new knot by pressing Shift and clicking a segment area.

A new knot will appear.

2   Remove a knot by selecting it and then pressing the Delete key or clicking the Delete Knot button.

You can modify a tangent in two ways: spline or linear. If you select the tangent, you can toggle between Spline (below, left) and Line mode (right).

3   Select all the knots on the shape and click the Spline/Line button to toggle to the Line setting.

In this example, all knots have been made linear.

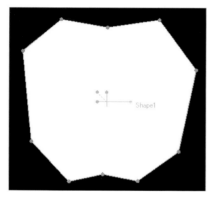

4   Click the Spline/Line button to return to the Spline setting.

5   Try breaking a tangent by Control-dragging on the end of it.

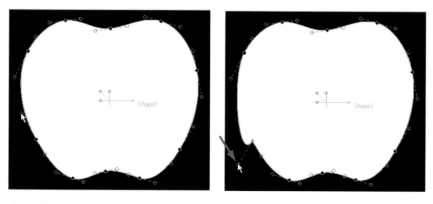

Control-drag the end tangent …   … to break it.

Once the tangent is broken, you can release the Control key.

6   Drag one of the two broken tangents and notice that the tangents are locked relative to each other.

To realign the tangents, press Shift and click the tangent end.

Creating and Modifying Shapes

You can create additional shapes by clicking the Add Shapes button.

1   Click the Add Shapes button.

This will put you automatically into Add Shapes mode, and you can add another shape.

2   Draw another shape and close it by clicking the first knot.

You can modify the shape by adjusting the transform control in the center of the shape. The small knobs going up and to the left are the Y and X scale parameters, respectively. The diagonal knot will scale both X and Y. The longer knob to the right will rotate it. Grabbing in the middle and dragging will move the shape.

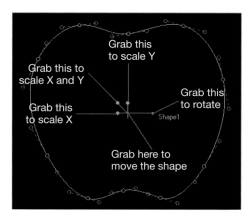

3   Experiment with the various shape transform controls.

TIP To move the transform control without modifying the shape, press Control and drag with the left mouse button.

Knot Modes

Four knot modes let you control the softness of a shape on a knot-by-knot basis, as described here:

Icon	Name	Hot Key	Action
Group mode	Group mode	F1	Moves both the main shape knot and the edge knot associated with it.
Main mode	Main mode	F2	Allows you to move only main shape knots; edge knots will not be modified.

Icon	Name	Hot Key	Action
Edge	Edge mode	F3	Moves only edges; you can therefore move the edge away from the shape.
Any	Any mode	F4	Allows you to pick any type of knot.

1   To create a soft edge, click the Edge mode icon and drag a knot out.

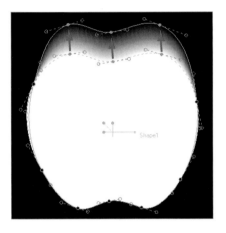

2   To reset the soft edge, right-click the edge knot and choose Reset Softedge.

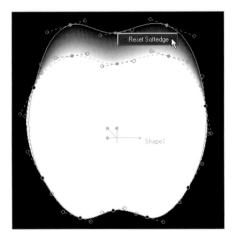

> **NOTE** ▶ Be careful with the soft edges. If you make a shape whose lines overlap, you may get rendering artifacts. To clean up minor artifacts, apply a slight blur with the Blur node.

3   Go back to Group mode.

Right Mouse Controls

The right mouse menu on a knot or transform control gives you several other options, such as move controls to change a shape's visibility and layering priority; set a shape's color options; copy, paste, and delete shapes; create parent-child relationships; and associate tracking information with points.

Right-Clicking a Knot

If you right-click a knot, you will see the following controls and commands.

The Bounding Box Toggle control, for example, gives you a box that can be transformed to both move and scale the shape. You don't need to choose this control; I just want you to know that it's there.

Another right mouse knot function allows you to make a shape black and then use it to punch a hole in other shapes.

1 Create a new shape.

2 Using the transform control, overlap the shapes.

3 Right-click one of the knots of an overlapping shape and choose Black.

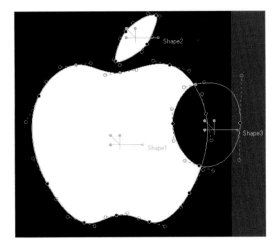

What do you know? The shape turned black.

The right mouse menu also has several Arrange commands, which can switch a shape's layering priority.

If you right-click the transform control, you can set up a parent-child relation-ship between your shapes.

1   Right-click the transform control of the shape that you want to be the parent, and choose Add Child.

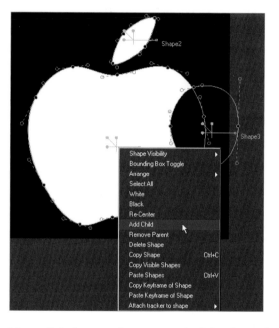

2   Next, click the transform control of the shape that you want to be the child.

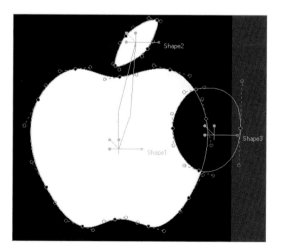

3   Now, move the parent shape, and then move the child shape.

When the parent is moved, the child follows, but the child can have motion independent of the parent.

4   Remove the parent-child relationship by right-clicking the child's transform control and choosing Remove Parent. (I wish I had that kind of control when I was a kid.)

TIP ▶ You may find that the transform control becomes uncentered from its shape depending on what actions you perform. If you right-click the transform control of a shape, you can choose Re-Center to center the transform control within the shape.

Roto Tips

Creating usable shape animations can be a bit tricky, the most common problem being edge chatter. Here are a few tips to help you on your way.

▶   Analyze the sequence. View your sequence to determine the frame that requires the greatest number of points to create the shape. It is easier to draw your shape on the most complex frame than to start on a simpler frame and add points later.

▶   Create shapes with fewer points. Use as many points as needed to create the shape, but avoid using more than necessary. The fewer the points, the easier it is to successfully animate the shape. Unnecessarily complex shapes are inevitably difficult to edit.

▶   Create multiple shapes. Draw multiple shapes and combine them into complex roto objects. Drawing separate shapes for the major parts of an object gives you finer control over motion, especially when separate objects intersect each other.

▶   Edit the shape in groups. Try not to individually move points in a shape unless absolutely necessary. Moving points in groups will maintain consistency and eliminate edge chatter.

▶ Keyframe, keyframe, keyframe. When you edit your shape at various frames in the sequence, Shake animates the shape between those keyframes. This saves you work. Make as few keyframes as possible, but include enough so that the shape properly follows the object that you are rotoing. For instance, on an 80-frame clip, start by adding keyframes at frames 1, 20, and 40. If more animation is needed, add keys at frames 10 and 30. Get the idea? Creating too many keyframes will cause the shape to jitter or chatter.

▶ Use a tracker. A Tracker, which is a node that analyzes the motion of a clip, can be attached to a shape or selected points. The motion from the Tracker is used to animate the horizontal and vertical positioning of the shape or point. It sure beats animating frame by frame. To attach a Tracker to a shape, right-click the shape transform control and choose Attach Tracker to Shape. To attach a Tracker to selected points, right-click one of the selected points and choose Attach Tracker to Selected Points. This calls up a list of pre-created Trackers for you to choose from. Tracking is covered in Lesson 7.

Creating a Rotoshape

Your mission, if you choose to accept it, is to create multiple animated roto-shapes of a woman walking in front of a car. The shapes that you create on a frame-by-frame basis will be used to place the woman in front of laser beams surrounding the car. This result of this roto exercise will be used in the MultiPlane lesson later in this book (Lesson 11).

1   Choose File > New Script and click No when prompted to save the script.

File	Edit	Tools	Viewers	R
New script				⌘N
Open script...				⌘O

2   FileIn the **woman** and **laser** clips from the Lesson04 folder.

3   Click the Fit Image to Viewer button to fit the image into the Viewer.

Let's start by doing a quick composite of these two images.

4   Click the **laser** clip once so that it is highlighted green.

5   From the Layer tab, select Over.

6   Connect the output of the **woman** clip into the right input of the Over node.

The laser beams are composited over the woman. Take a look at the composite in a flipbook.

7   On the Globals tab, click the Auto button to the right of the timeRange button.

8 Click the Home button at the bottom-right corner of the interface.

The Time Bar is automatically set to the Globals timeRange.

9 Click the Flipbook icon.

As you can see, the laser beams are in front of the woman but should be behind her. To isolate and place her in front of the lasers, create a shape around her body.

10 Close the flipbook when you are done playing the clip.

11 From the Image tab, select a RotoShape node.

12 Click the left side of the **woman** clip so that you can view it while drawing the shape.

It will be helpful to set the resolution of the RotoShape node to be the same as the **woman** clip.

13 In the RotoShape1 node, set the Res parameters to 960x540.

I have no idea how this clip ended up at this bizarre resolution. But hey, did I mention that Shake is resolution independent?

14 Go to frame 1 and click the AutoKey button under the Viewer.

TIP There's nothing worse than rotoing a shape when you've forgotten to turn on the keyframe mode. Turning on the keyframe mode by clicking the AutoKey button ensures that any changes you make to your shape will be animated over time.

At this point, you have a choice. You can either create one very complex shape around the woman, or create a number of less complex ones. What is the right way to do this? For those who chose one complex shape, I say get out of my sight. The rest of you can stay and play. Using one complex shape would become very difficult to deal with because of the motion of the woman's legs. The best way to roto this shot is to break the roto into individual shapes—one for the head and arms (since they are not moving), one for the torso, and one for each leg.

15 At frame 1, draw a shape around the woman's head and arms.

16 Close the shape by clicking the first knot.

Your shape should look something like this:

17 Rename the RotoShape1 node *Head_and_Arms*.

You need to create three additional RotoShape nodes.

18 On the Image tab, click the RotoShape icon three times.

19 Set the Res parameters to 960x540 in each of the new RotoShape nodes and rename them *Torso, Right_Leg,* and *Left_Leg.*

20 View the **woman** clip by clicking its left side, and edit the Torso node by clicking its right side.

21 Draw a shape around the woman's torso.

22 Click the right side of the Left_Leg node to edit it, and draw a shape around her left leg.

23 Click the right side of the Right_Leg node, and draw a shape around her right leg.

24 You will need to adjust the shape every four frames or so.

Create as few keyframes as possible to animate the shapes, but enough so that the shapes properly follow the object. I like to set keyframes every eight frames or so, on frames 8, 16, 24, and so on. If I need more keyframes, I go back and set them every fourth frame by adding keyframes at 4, 12, 20, and so on.

25 Continue to adjust the various shapes, being mindful to first click the right side of the particular RotoShape node that you want to adjust.

For your reference, or if you just like cheating, I have prepared a script of this exercise. You can use it as a reference and see where I have set keyframes.

26 To see my script, choose File > Add Script, and select **woman_roto.shk** from the Lesson04 folder.

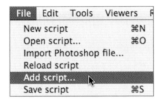

Add Script adds to your current script. Feel free to compare it with what you have done so far.

TIP If at any time the transform controls get in your way, Control-click and drag to move them.

OK, it is hours later and you are finished rotoing the woman using multiple shapes. To see how well you have done, combine the various RotoShape nodes into one matte.

27 Highlight the Heads_and_Arms node and select MultiLayer from the Layer tab.

This MultiLayer node accepts an infinite number of input images, each layer containing its own unique settings to control compositing mode, opacity, and channels. It is handy for putting together all of the RotoShape nodes.

28 Drag the outputs of the Torso, Left_Leg, and Right_Leg nodes to the plus sign (+) on the top of the MultiLayer1 node that appears when the cursor passes over it.

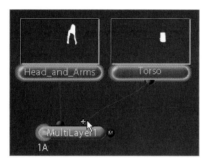

29 Create a flipbook of MultiLayer1, play the sequence, and close when done.

Because the image that you are rotoing is moving, it could benefit from a motion blur. Motion blur is the apparent blurring of moving objects while the camera shutter is open, creating the illusion of movement. Without motion blur, rapidly moving objects appear to strobe.

30 Position the Time Bar at frame 30.

31 Double-click the Left_Leg node and set the Motion Blur parameter to a value of 1.

Motion blur is added to the left leg.

32 Do the same for each of the other RotoShape nodes.

Now, make a flipbook of the MultiLayer1 node to see the added motion blur on the moving shapes.

33 Double-click the MultiLayer1 node, click the Flipbook icon, and play the sequence.

34 When you're done, close the flipbook.

Integrating Rotoshapes into the Composite

You are now ready to integrate your rotoshapes into your composite.

1 Go to frame 23 and double-click the Over1 node to view and edit it.

2 Click the **laser** clip once to highlight it, and select Outside from the Layer tab.

The Outside function places one image outside the mask of a second image. Only the mask of the second image is considered in the composite, while the color comes from the foreground image. This is a great tool to mask layers. Essentially, the mask created by all of the RotoShape nodes is used to cut a hole in the **laser** clip, but only in the area of the mask.

3   Connect the output of the MultiLayer1 node to the right input of Outside1.

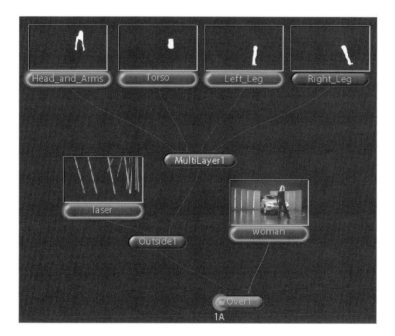

The laser beams are now placed behind the woman.

4   Make a flipbook of Over1.

5   Evaluate the flipbook frame by frame using the left and right arrow keys.

6   Make notes as to which frames need further adjustment.

7   Close the flipbook and edit the various rotoshapes as needed.

8   Continue until you are satisfied with the edges around the woman where the laser beams cross over her.

When you are satisfied with your work, render the result of the MultiLayer1 node.

9   Click the MultiLayer1 node once to select it.

10 Right-click the FileOut node on the Image tab and choose Branch.

11 When the File Browser opens, go to your home directory and select the Shake_Output folder that you created in Lesson 2.

12 Enter a filename, *woman_roto.#.iff*, at the bottom of the File Browser and click OK.

13 Right-click the woman_roto node and choose Render > Render FileOut Nodes from the pop-up menu.

14 When the Render Parameters window opens, click Render.

The Monitor window appears and shows the progress of your render.

15 Compare your version with my version. What do you think? Whose version is better? Well, thank you. I appreciate that. You are so kind.

16 Quit Shake.

Rotoshape animation is an essential skill for every compositor, as most large postproduction companies have dedicated artists to create animated mattes. As a roto artist in training, you have gained valuable knowledge. You might even be able to make some money.

Miscellaneous RotoShape Viewer Controls

Button	Name	Action
	Toggle Fill/No Fill Mode	Quickly toggles the rendering of the shape on and off.
	Show/Hide Tangents	Controls the tangent visibility. When in Pick mode, only the active knot displays a tangent; None hides all tangents; All displays all tangents.
	Lock/Unlock Tangents	Locks or unlocks the tangents of adjacent knots when moving any knot.

Button	Name	Action
	Enable/Disable Transform	A really annoying control to pan the entire collection of shapes; it is off by default.
	Key Single/Multiple Shapes	Indicates whether you are keyframing the active shape or all shapes when you roto.
	Toggle Path	If the main onscreen transform tool is turned on, this toggles the visibility of the animation path; it doesn't have a purpose if the tool is turned off.
	Enable/Disable Shape Transform Control	Turns the shape transform control on and off.
	Import/Export Shapes	Imports and exports shapes.

The Import Shapes button can be used to import shapes from programs such as SilhouetteFX's Roto, available at www.silhouettefx.com.

Lesson Review

1. What is rotoscoping?
2. What does the Toggle Fill/No Fill mode button do?
3. What are the four knot modes and how are they used?
4. When and why would you use a motion blur effect?
5. How many keyframes are needed to animate a shape?

Answers

1. Rotoscoping is a frame-by-frame shape-drawing technique used to create animated shapes over time.

2. The Toggle Fill/No Fill mode button toggles the rendering of shapes on and off.

3. The four knot modes are Group, Main, Edge, and Any, and they are used to control softness of a shape on a knot-by-knot basis.

4. Motion blur is used to reduce strobing and to smooth out moving objects.

5. You should create as few keyframes as possible to animate the shape, but enough so that the shape follows the object properly.

5

Lesson 5
Color Correction

Color correction is a generic term for any process that alters the perceived color of an image. The mere mention of the words sends shivers up my spine, because no two people can ever agree on what looks right, including your clients. The perception of color will no doubt be different for every person who looks at your monitor. So, charge by the hour and color correction will be your friend. Fortunately, Shake provides you with a vast array of color-manipulation tools with which to drive up your profits.

The Shake Color tab.

Basic Color-Correction Tools

In Shake, color is typically described in an RGB range between 0 and 1. The color nodes are generally either mathematical corrections to color (for example, adding .5 to the red channel) or the rearranging of specific color channels.

Many of the color-correction nodes can have identical results. For example, Mult and Brightness are the same command, except Brightness affects all three RGB channels at the same time, whereas Mult allows you to adjust each channel individually. Other functions such as Lookup and ColorX can also duplicate most of the other color nodes. Although ColorX is the most powerful and complicated node on the Color tab, it is also the slowest because it acts on each individual pixel.

Shake's basic color correctors are split up into nodes that can be rearranged in any fashion you wish. The basic nodes are as follows:

▶ Add—The Add function adds to the R, G, B, or A channel. It will also add color to black areas, including those beyond the image frame, in case you move the image later on.

▶ Brightness—This function is simply a multiplier on the RGB channels and is useful for brightening or darkening an image.

▶ ContrastLum—ContrastLum applies a contrast change to the image, with a smooth falloff on both the low and high ends.

▶ Gamma—A gamma correction affects only the midtones while retaining the black and white values of an image. Pixels with a value of 0 or 1 are unaffected. Only nonblack and nonwhite pixels are adjusted.

▶ Mult—This function multiplies the R, G, B, or A channel. Unlike Add, the Mult operator does not add color to black areas.

▶ Lookup—This performs an arbitrary lookup on the image. It is extremely flexible, allowing you to mimic most other color-correction nodes. It's also handy for adjusting color values using a curve.

▶ Reorder—The Reorder operator lets you shuffle channels. The argument to this command specifies the new order. A channel can be copied to several different channels.

Using the Color Nodes

It's time to try out a few of the color nodes.

1 Open Shake.

2 Choose File > Open Script.

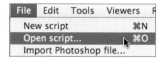

3 Go to the Lesson05 folder and load the `color1.shk` script.

This script has a space shuttle image connected to some basic color-correction nodes.

4 Double-click the Add1 node.

You'll see a + next to the Color parameter. This means that additional parameters can be viewed.

5 Click the + next to the Color parameter.

This reveals a row of radio buttons with another + at the far left.

6 Click the + next to the R radio button.

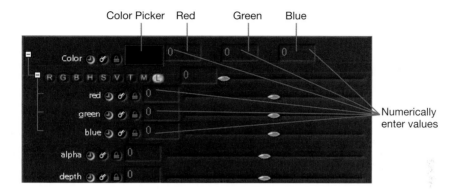

When tuning parameters within the color nodes, you can choose several methods:

▶ Enter numeric values in the RGB text fields.

▶ Drag the slider next to each text field.

▶ Click the color swatch and select a color from the Color Picker.

▶ Use keyboard shortcuts: If you press the keyboard character *R* (red), *G* (green), *B* (blue), *H* (hue), *S* (saturation), *V* (value), *L* (luminance), *M* (magenta), or *T* (temperature) and drag left and right in the Parameters workspace, you will modify that parameter.

▶ To gang up the Red, Green, and Blue sliders, press V (value) and drag left and right.

7 Press the R key and drag to the right in the Parameters workspace.

This will add to the red channel.

8 Once you have added red, press the H key and drag left and right.

This shifts the hue of the color. Modifying using this method modifies only the color that is added, multiplied, and so on. For example, dragging a color while pressing S (saturation), will decrease not the saturation of the image but rather the saturation of the color that you are adding to the image.

9 View and edit each of the other color nodes attached to the takeoff node by double-clicking them. Go ahead and experiment by adjusting each node's parameters to see how it affects the image.

10 Now double-click the Reorder1 node.

The Reorder function allows you to easily move an image's channels around.

11 To copy the red channel to all three channels while leaving the alpha alone, type *rrra* in the Channels parameter.

All three color channels come from the red channel.

12 View each color channel, ending with the alpha channel in the Viewer, by clicking the View RGBA Channels button.

13 To remove the alpha channel, type *rgbn* in the Channels parameter.

The alpha channel turns black.

14 To copy the luminance into the alpha channel, type *rgbl*.

The letter *l* refers to luminance, which is the average luminance of the color channels.

15 Press the C key in the Viewer to show the RGB channels.

These are just the basic color-correction tools in Shake; many more are located on the Color tab.

Using PlotScanline to Understand Color Corrections

To help you better understand some of Shake's color-correction functions, a useful operator called PlotScanline is included. It looks at a single horizontal scan line of an image and plots the brightness of a pixel for each X location. This lets you graphically see how a color-correction node is affecting the image.

1   Choose File > New Script.

2   Click No when prompted whether to save the current script.

3   Select the Ramp node in the Image tab.

4   Set the Res parameters to *256* by *256*.

The ramp is 256 pixels wide and ranges in value from 0 to 1. This provides a 1:1 correspondence between the range of possible values in an 8-bit image.

5 Add PlotScanline from the Other tab after Ramp1, and make sure that the Res parameters are set to 256x256.

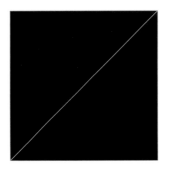

The PlotScanline curve indicates that this is a linear ramp.

6 Now insert a color-correction operator, such as ContrastLum, from the Color tab into the chain, after Ramp1 and before PlotScanline1.

7 Set the Value parameter to *1.5* and the softClip parameter to *1.0*.

That will modify the gradient, and the plot will reflect this. As you adjust the values of your contrast, the plot updates to reflect any changes.

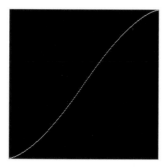

The image is effectively a plot of the Contrast function.

8 View Ramp1, ContrastLum1, and PlotScanline1 in turn to see how the adjustment affects the image.

PlotScanline can also graph the different channels of an image separately.

9 Replace ContrastLum1 with a Gamma node located on the Color tab.

10 Adjust the rGamma, gGamma, and bGamma parameters so that they are different values.

There are now three curves representing red, green, and blue values.

11 Replace Gamma1 with different color nodes and see how PlotScanline reacts as the various parameters are adjusted.

Concatenation

A unique aspect of Shake's color handling is that it concatenates color corrections. This means that if you have ten color operations in a row, Shake mathematically compiles them into one operation. You don't have to spend the time processing the ten nodes, just one. An important second benefit is that if you darken an image by half and then double its brightness, the adjustments cancel each other out, leaving no change. Without this functionality, you would be throwing data away when you darken the image, and you wouldn't be able to recover it by brightening it in a second operation.

The following functions concatenate:

▶ Add

▶ Brightness

▶ Clamp

▶ ColorMatch

▶ Compress

▶ ContrastRGB (but not ContrastLum)

▶ DelogC

▶ Expand

▶ Fade

▶ Gamma

▶ Invert

▶ LogC

▶ Lookup

▶ Lookup File

▶ Mult

▶ Set

▶ Solarize

▶ Threshold

Furthermore, AdjustHSV and LookupHSV concatenate only with each other. If you have a hard time remembering which nodes concatenate with each other, you can tell by the C in the top-left corner of a node. If it has a C, it concatenates with other nodes that show a C.

NOTE ▶ Concatenation occurs only on adjacent nodes. If you attach a different class of node between two nodes that concatenate with each other, it will break the concatenation.

Color Matching Using Channel Isolation

Very often, you will encounter two images from the same location that are not color matched. By looking at the individual color channels in the Viewer, you can easily color-match these types of shots.

1   Choose File > New Script and click No when prompted whether to save your script.

2   FileIn the **florida_cu.0001.iff** and **florida_ms.0001.iff** clips from the Lesson05 folder.

3   Double-click each clip to view them individually.

4   You may need to click the Fit Image to Viewer button to see the entire picture.

These are two aerial views of Florida with different framing and color correction. You will cut out a portion of the **florida_cu** clip, color-correct it, and composite it over the **florida_ms** clip. You'll start by using a RotoShape node to create the cutout.

5   Select RotoShape from the Image tab and click the left side of the
     florida_cu clip so that it can be viewed.

6   Set the Res parameters to *1920* by *1080*.

7   Draw a shape that looks approximately like the one below.

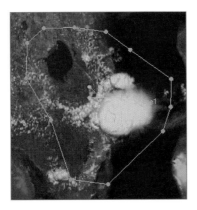

8   Click the Edge icon and drag from the various points to create a soft edge.

     This will help blend the two images together.

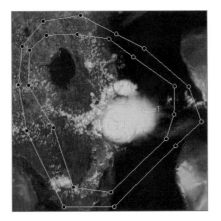

9   Click the **florida_cu** clip and select SwitchMatte from the Layer tab.

SwitchMatte copies a channel from the second image into the matte channel of the first image.

10   Connect the output of the RotoShape1 node to the second output of the SwitchMatte1 node.

The cutout can now be composited over the wider shot.

11   Select Over from the Layer tab and connect **florida_ms** to the right input.

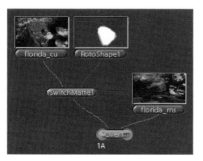

The trick now will be to exactly match the size of the **florida_cu** clip.

12   Select the SwitchMatte1 node and insert a Move2D node from the Transform tab.

You could drive yourself crazy adjusting the position and scaling manually, or you could use the nifty alignment technique shown in the following steps.

13   Add an Invert node from the Color tab and a Mix node from the Layer tab after the Move2D1 node.

14 Connect the output of the **florida_ms** node into the right input of Mix1.

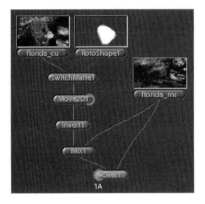

15 Click the left side of Mix1 to load it into the Viewer, and click the right side of the Move2D1 node to load it into the Parameters tab.

The Move2D onscreen controls appear.

The combination of Invert and Mix lets you clearly see the differences between the two images. When you adjust the Move2D1controls, the image will turn gray where it is aligned exactly. Because our two images have obvious differences (one has clouds), the aligned result will never look completely gray.

16 Adjust the Move2D1 controls until the images are aligned as well as possible.

Your final alignment will look something like this.

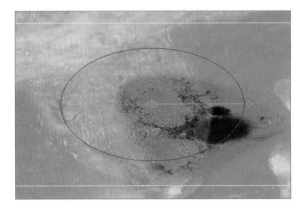

In case you are curious, I used the following settings to achieve the alignment: xPan = 136.8; yPan = 51.7; xScale = .4115; yScale = .2503.

Since the images are aligned, the Invert and Mix nodes can be deactivated, as they are no longer needed.

17 Drag a box around the Invert1 and Mix1 nodes to select them, and press the I key to ignore the nodes.

18 Double-click the Over1 node to view it.

The composite looks good except for the color correction of the inserted element. We will use a Mult node to adjust it.

19 Insert a Mult node from the Color tab between florida_cu and SwitchMatte1.

20 Expand the color channels by first clicking the + next to the Color parameter and then the + next to the R button.

21 In the Viewer, look only at the blue channel. You can do this by placing the pointer over the Viewer and pressing the B key.

By isolating individual color channels, it is easier to match the colors.

22 Zoom in to the area that you are color-correcting, and adjust the Blue slider until the **florida_cu** cutout matches the background.

You may find it difficult to match the two images exactly using the slider. You can adjust the Blue parameter with more accuracy by using the "virtual" sliders, which change the value interactively and give you finer control—left-drag lowers the value, right-drag raises the value. The virtual sliders are activated when you Control-drag in a Color parameter box.

23 Control-drag the Blue field to adjust it with the virtual slide.

TIP ▶ Set your Update mode to Always. As you drag a parameter, Shake is constantly rendering. This makes the color adjustments more interactive.

24 In the Viewer, look only at the red channel.

25 Control-drag the Red field to adjust it.

26 In the Viewer, look only at the green channel.

27 Adjust the Green parameter until the `florida_cu` cutout matches the background.

I set the Red, Green, and Blue parameters to: 1.2, 1.1, and 1.5, respectively.

28 Now look at the RGB channels in the Viewer at the same time.

If you zoom out, you'll see that the background clip is softer than the `florida_cu` cutout. To finish the composite, we'll use a Blur node.

29 Add a Blur node after Move2D1 and set the pixels to *5, 5*.

The two images are now matched perfectly (depending on your standards) to the background. Another way to color-match the two shots would be to use the ColorMatch node, explained in the following section.

Color Matching Using ColorMatch

ColorMatch lets you apply a color correction to an image by taking an old set of colors (source color) and matching them to a new set (destination color) by adjusting the low, middle, and high values of the image. You can also do Contrast, Gamma, Mult, and Add color corrections.

When you match color using the Color Picker, a good workflow strategy is to first select all three source colors, and then select the destination colors. Otherwise, you may pick colors that have been modified.

> **TIP** Another technique to use when you're scrubbing is to ignore the node while scrubbing (select the node and press I in Node View) and then turn it on when you're finished.

Let's try to match the Florida shots using the ColorMatch node.

1   Extract the Mult1 node by highlighting it and pressing the E key.

    This automatically extracts the node from the tree.

2   Place a ColorMatch node after florida_cu.

3   Double-click ColorMatch1 to make it the active node.

    You'll start by selecting the low, mid, and high source colors.

4   Click the Color Picker tab in the Node workspace.

The Color Picker, which is in a tab on the Node workspace, allows you to sample values from the Viewer, and then drag and drop them onto other parameters. It includes handy analysis tools for finding and comparing different color values on your image. You can examine minimum, average, current, and maximum pixel values, which is particularly useful, naturally, when doing color corrections.

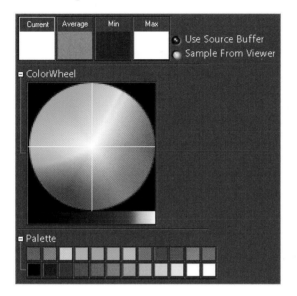

5   Drag across the image.

As you drag, the image's values will appear in the Color Picker, interactively updating the Min, Max, Average, and Current color boxes.

In matching the two Florida shots, the first step is to choose the shadows, or darkest areas of the screen.

6   Zoom in to the middle of Florida near the lake and the hurricane by pressing the + key repeatedly.

7 Drag the pointer over the dark area of water above the hurricane.

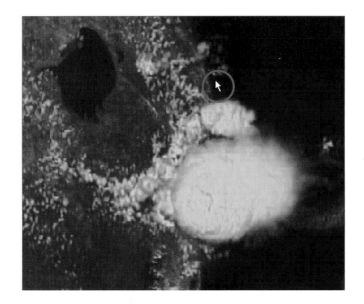

You've sampled a color—now what? Make it the ColorMatch1 lowSource color.

8 Click the Current color box once to select it.

9 Drag the Current color box in the Color Picker onto the color swatch next to lowSource in ColorMatch1.

Now you can set the midSource and highSource values.

10 Click the midSource color swatch.

When you click a color swatch in a node's parameters, the Color Picker will open automatically, or become active if it's already open. When you pick a color from the Viewer, it will be entered as a parameter value automatically.

11 Select the midSource color according to the following picture:

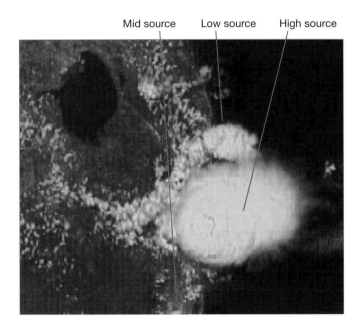

Mid source   Low source   High source

12 Click the highSource color swatch and select the highSource color according to the preceding picture.

Now that the source colors are selected, you can select the destination colors.

13 Change the Node workspace from the Color Picker to the Node View.

14 Click the left side of the Over1 node so that you can sample colors while viewing the composite.

15 Select the mid, low, and high destination colors. For each selection, click and drag in the area shown in the figure below until the colors match.

Mid source   Low source   High source

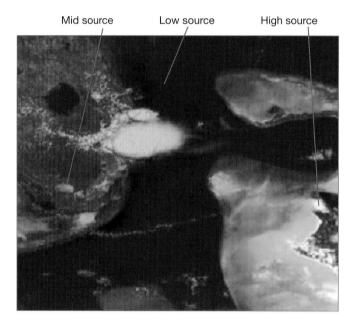

If you are in Update Always mode, the color correction happens interactively. Once it matches visually, you can stop dragging the pointer.

Your final image should look like this:

The ColorCorrect Node

ColorCorrect combines Add, Mult, Gamma, ContrastRGB, ColorReplace, Invert, Reorder, and Lookup into one node, giving you the ability to tune the image in only the shadow, midtone, or highlight areas. ColorCorrect will also give your clients all of the needed controls to endlessly noodle with your shots. Not to worry; you are charging by the hour, remember?

NOTE ▶ ColorCorrect will break concatenation with connecting color corrections.

1   Choose File > New Script and click No when prompted whether to save your script.

2   FileIn the **porthole.0001.iff** clip from the Lesson05 folder.

3   Click the Fit Image to Viewer button under the Viewer so that you can see the entire image.

4   Attach a ColorCorrect node from the Color tab.

ColorCorrect Subtabs

The ColorCorrect node is organized into the following seven subtabs:

Subtab	Action
Master	Applies the correction to the entire image.
Low Controls	Applies the correction primarily to the darkest portion of the image with the correction falling off as the image gets brighter.
Mid Controls	Applies the correction primarily to the middle range of the image.
High Controls	Applies the correction primarily to the highlights of the image, with falloff as the image gets darker.
Curves	Applies manual correction to the image using curves.
Misc	Performs secondary color correction, as well as Invert, Reorder, and preMultiplied control.
Range Curves	Displays the different image ranges (shadows, midtones, highlights), their control curves, and the final concatenated curve of the color correction.

Master, Low, Mid, and High Controls

The first four tabs are identical except for the portion of the image that they let you modify. Each has controls to Add, multiply (Gain), and apply a Gamma to the RGB channels, as well as to apply contrast on a per-channel basis (Contrast, Center, and SoftClip).

Buttons at the bottom of the tab let you toggle between RGB display and other color models. You can switch between RGB, HSV, HLS, CMY, and TMV (Temperature/Magenta-Cyan/Value).

1 Click the HSV button at the bottom of the tab.

The numbers are converted to HSV space.

2   Switch back to RGB mode by clicking the RGB button.

Each color value has an AutoKey and a View Curves button associated with all three channels for that parameter. All three channels are treated equally.

NOTE ▶ When ColorCorrect is saved into a script, the values are always stored in RGB space.

Working with Low, Mid, and High Ranges

Here is the difference when working with Low, Mid, and High. This is the original image:

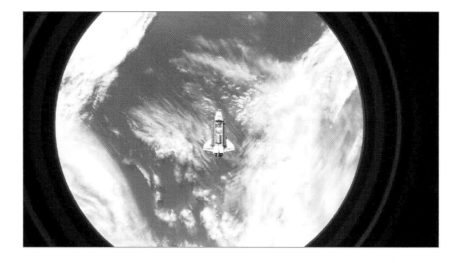

1   Click the Mid Controls tab in the ColorCorrect1 node.

2   Adjust the Blue Gain to *1.5*.

Blue is added only to the midtones of the image, which in this case is primarily the ocean.

3   Select the High Controls tab.

4   Adjust the Blue Gain to a value of *0.75*.

Only the highlights of this image are adjusted, which makes the clouds a warm yellow color. You can also control the range of the image's shadows, midtones, and highlights by going to the Range Curves tab.

5   Select the Range Curves tab.

This tab displays your final color correction, as well as the Low, Mid, and High mask ranges, as curves. You can also use the display to switch the output from the normal, corrected image to a display of the low areas, the mid areas, or the high areas. A color display was used rather than one based on luminance, because different channels have different values.

6   Click the View L, View M, and View H buttons.

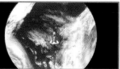

       View L   View M   View H

7 To control the mask areas, turn off the Colors display and turn on the Ranges display at the bottom of the Range Curves tab.

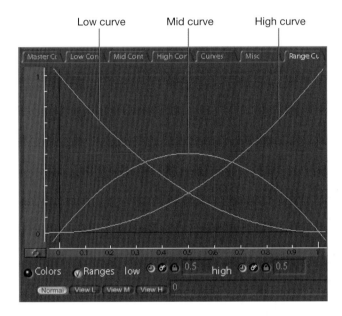

Here are the curves for the low, mid, and high values. These curves can be modified by adjusting the low and high parameters.

8 Right-click the Parameters workspace and select Reset All Values.

Curves Tab

The Curves tab lets you apply manual modifications to the lookup curve by mapping input colors to output colors.

1 Click the Curves tab.

2 Click the bExpr radio button.

3 Insert some new knots (or points) by Shift-clicking a segment of the curve and dragging the newly created points to correct the image.

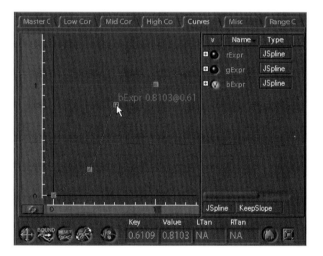

Color correcting using curves can yield results that are hard to duplicate with any other method.

Misc Tab

1 Choose File > New Script, and click No when prompted whether to save your script.

2 FileIn the **fish.0001.iff** clip from the Lesson05 folder.

3 Attach the **fish** clip to a ColorCorrect node.

4 Click the Misc tab.

This Misc tab has several functions:

▶ Invert—Inverts the red, green, and blue channels.

▶ reorderChannels—By entering a string, you can swap or remove your channels according to the standard Reorder method.

▶ preMultiplied—Toggle this on if your image is premultiplied (typically, an image coming from a computer-generated render), and this function will insert an MDiv before the calculations and an MMult afterward.

▶ Color Replace—This is the same as the ColorReplace node located on the Color tab. It lets you isolate a color according to its hue, saturation, and value, and replace it with a different color. Other areas of the spectrum will remain unchanged. This is especially handy for spill suppression during keying operations.

NOTE ▶ There is a toggle to affect the alpha channel in the standalone ColorReplace node in case you also want to pull a mask of the affected source color.

Next, you will isolate and replace the fish's blue border.

5 Click the Source color swatch.

6 Click the bright blue part of the fish near the large yellow rear fin.

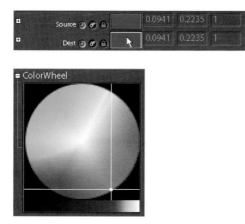

7 Now click the Destination color swatch and choose a shade of magenta from the Color Picker.

The areas of the fish that were blue have only partially turned magenta. If you adjust some of the Range/Falloff parameters, you can get it just right.

8   Adjust the satRange to a value of *0* and satFalloff to a value of *0.6*.

The blue areas of the fish should now look completely magenta.

9   Quit Shake.

Lesson Review

1.   What does the PlotScanline tool do?

2.   What is concatenation and why is it useful?

3.   What is the Color Picker?

4.   What does the ColorReplace function do and where is it located?

Answers

1. The PlotScanline tool provides a graphical representation of a color operation.

2. When you have multiple adjacent color operations, Shake mathematically compiles them into a single operation. This is called *concatenation*, and it is useful because you only have to spend the time processing a single operation.

3. The Color Picker is a tab in the Node workspace you can use to select colors. It includes handy analysis tools for finding and comparing different color values in an image.

4. The ColorReplace function lets you replace one color with another. It is available in the Misc subtab of the ColorCorrect node as well as in the Color tool tab.

Keyboard Shortcuts

Color Correcting

R-drag	adjusts red
G-drag	adjusts green
B-drag	adjusts blue
H-drag	adjusts hue
S-drag	adjusts saturation
V-drag	adjusts value
L-drag	adjusts luminance
C-drag	adjusts cyan
M-drag	adjusts magenta
Y-drag	adjusts yellow
T-drag	adjusts temperature

6

Lesson Files

Media
surf.1-50.iff

wall.0001.tif

wire1.1-10.iff

wire1_clean.1-10.iff

wire1_final.1-10.iff

wire2.1-30.iff

wire2_final.1-30.iff

wire3.1-15.iff

wire3_final.1-15.iff

Time
This lesson takes approximately 2½ hours to complete.

Goals
Recognize the basic functions of the QuickPaint node

Use QuickPaint to scrawl like a monkey

Create a write-on effect

Rotoscope and remove dust from a sequence of images

AutoAlign a clean plate to a moving image

Remove wires from an image using the Clone and Reveal brushes

QuickPaint

QuickPaint is a simple touch-up tool that helps you fix minor problems such as holes in a matte or dirt on your image. It is a procedural paint node that allows you to change strokes after they have been drawn. Think of it as just another compositing tool that can easily be used in conjunction with other Shake nodes. That means you can apply the effect and easily ignore it, remove it, or reorder it after you have applied your paint strokes. It is very useful, but it is not intended to act as a full-featured, matte painting package. Now that your expectations have been sufficiently lowered, you can begin.

Setting Resolution

You can apply a QuickPaint node to another node, or you can create a floating paint node to apply later to a different node with a layer or mask operator. When the node is floating, it takes the resolution of the default width and height.

> **TIP** A good way to set the resolution is to create a Color node and attach the QuickPaint node to it. You then set the resolution in the Color node on the image tab. When you are using the Color node, keep in mind that the alpha channel is set to 1—completely opaque—by default. Keep your resolution in mind, because QuickPaint does not paint beyond the boundaries of the frame.

1   Open Shake.

2   On the Image tab, select a QuickPaint node.

The first input of the node is for the background and also acts as the Clone source. The second input is for the Reveal source.

Edit vs. Paint Mode

The QuickPaint node has a tool shelf on the Viewer, and three subtabs—Paint Controls, Edit Controls, and Paint Globals—in the Parameters workspace.

The first button on the Viewer is the Paint/Edit toggle.

When you are in Paint mode, you can apply new brush strokes, and the Paint Controls subtab will be at the front in the Parameters workspace.

When in Edit mode, you can modify either your current stroke or any previous stroke.

You can control the paint characteristics (color, size, brush type, opacity, and softness), modify the position or shape of the stroke, or apply a write-on/off effect.

When you are in Edit mode, the Edit Controls subtab will be at the front. If you switch to the Edit Controls subtab, the Viewer will also switch to the Edit tab. The same switch occurs with the Paint mode, but you can also quickly switch into Paint mode by selecting a brush type in the Viewer.

If you are in Edit mode, you can select any stroke to modify by clicking the invisible stroke, which makes the stroke appear. You can also adjust the strokeIndex slider to expose previous strokes numerically.

Using the Brushes

The different brushes can paint on all of the image's channels at once or on the individual red, green, blue, or alpha channels separately using the R, G, B, and

A buttons. For example, if you wanted to touch up only an alpha channel, you would turn off the RGB channels.

There are five basic brush types, with one modifier to change the drop-off on any of those types.

The basic paint tools are as follows:

Button	Name	Action
	Hard/Soft toggle	Paints any brush type with a soft falloff; it isn't a brush, it just modifies other brushes.
	Hard/Soft toggle	Paints any brush type with a hard falloff.
	Paint brush	Applies RGBA color to the first input.
	Smudge brush	Smears pixels around; always use the Hard/Soft toggle's hard setting with this tool.
	Eraser brush	Erases previously applied paint strokes only, without affecting the background image.
	Reveal brush	Exposes whatever is in the second image input; if no second image input exists, it acts as an Outside node, punching a hole through both the paint and the first input source.
	Clone brush	Copies from whatever is created by the paint node or whatever comes from the first image input; to move the brush target relative to the source, use Shift-drag.

1   Make sure you are in Paint mode, and select the Paint brush.

2   OK, now you can paint. Just don't make a mess.

3   To control the brush size, use Control-drag. You can set the size numerically in the Parameters workspace as well.

Here's a little something I sketched up in five minutes:

OK, I am not really that good at painting with a mouse, but some of you
no doubt will already have a masterpiece on the screen.

Choosing a Color

You can choose your paint color and opacity in several different ways.

In the Parameters workspace is the Color Picker. Use it in the standard way to
select your color, either from the color wheel, or by picking a color from the

image. You can also press *P* on the keyboard to temporarily jump into Color Pick mode.

NOTE ▶ The Color swatch on the Viewer indicates only the currently selected color.

Modifying Strokes

You can animate strokes by using the Interpolation or Frame setting, or you can modify any stroke after it has been made by switching to Edit mode. To switch to Edit mode, either click the Paint/Edit toggle or go to the Edit Controls subtab.

Once in Edit mode, you can select a stroke in one of three ways:

▶ Clicking the stroke—The stroke will have an onscreen control drawn on it.

▶ Selecting the strokeIndex in the Edit Controls subtab—Each stroke is assigned a number, which can be accessed by the strokeIndex.

▶ Clicking the History Steps buttons—You can use these buttons to move backward or forward through your paint stroke history. This will not only select the stroke, but also draw up to that stroke. Even though the history list may contain a full range of strokes, later strokes are not drawn until you step to them by clicking the forward History Steps button.

1   Toggle QuickPaint to Edit mode.

2   Click the History Steps back button (minus sign) to cycle backward through your previous paint strokes.

You can select knots or points on the stroke with the standard method of Shift-drag to add to your active knots, or Control-drag to remove from your active knots. You can also simply select a knot and drag it.

3   Select some of the knots on a stroke.

Once you have selected the knots, you can move them around and use the standard AutoKey controls if you want to set keyframes. You can drag the knots in one of two ways. If you are in Linear Move mode, the knots will all move the same distance. If you are in Weighted Move mode, the knots nearest the cursor will move the most. (This does not apply when only one knot is selected.) You can also activate this mode temporarily by holding down the Z key and dragging. Using these tools, you can animate your strokes.

—— Linear Move mode

—— Weighted Move mode

4   Experiment with both Linear Move and Weighted Move modes while moving a selection of knots.

If you ever want to delete a stroke, you can do so by clicking the Erase Last Stroke icon.

Sadly, QuickPaint and Undo are not on good terms, and as a result, Undo does not work with QuickPaint. Thus, you have the Erase Last

Stroke feature. You can also use the Edit Controls subtab to modify
your strokes.

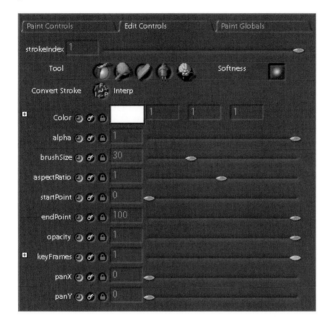

With the Edit Controls subtab, you can switch the brush type simply
by clicking one of the Tool buttons at the top of the tab. You can also
change the softness. Additionally, you can alter the color, alpha, opacity,
brush size, or aspect ratio of the current stroke, all of which can also be
animated.

5   Click the New Canvas icon to remove all strokes from your canvas.

If you can't see the New Canvas icon, you may need to expand the
Viewer area.

Understanding Stroke Modes

You can use any of three different stroke modes while painting: Frame, Interpolate, or Persist. You will use these different modes throughout the course of this lesson.

▶ Frame—When you paint in this mode, you are painting only on the current frame.

▶ Interp—When in this mode, you can interpolate your brushstrokes. Go to frame 1 and paint a stroke. Now go to, say, frame 20 and paint. When you drag back between frames 1 and 20 on the Time Bar, the stroke interpolates. If you go beyond frame 20 or before frame 1, the image is black. To insert a second interpolation stroke, toggle through the modes until you reach Interp again, and use the strokeIndex slider to select the stroke you want to modify.

▶ Persist—In this mode, the stroke persists from frame to frame. You can change it by going into Edit mode and animating it, but otherwise it will not change.

Converting Strokes

So far you have been painting in the Frame mode, which is the default. You can convert paint strokes in the Edit Controls subtab by clicking the Convert Stroke icon. For example, you can convert a stroke created in Frame mode to a stroke that persists from frame to frame.

Interpolating Paint Strokes

In this example, you will create a paint stroke at frame 1 and another at frame 50 in Frame mode. The strokes will be converted to Interp(olate) mode, and Shake will transition from one stroke to another.

1   Click the Paint brush icon to go back to Paint mode.

2   Make sure that Frame mode is enabled.

3   At frame 1, draw the number *2*.

4   At frame 50, draw a *5*.

NOTE ▶ In these images, each number is drawn as a single stroke.

5 Click the Edit Controls subtab.

6 Click the Convert Stroke icon.

The Convert stroke window appears.

7 In the Convert stroke window, enable Interp.

8 Enter *1, 2* in the Stroke Range field and click OK.

This instructs Shake to combine paint strokes 1 and 2 into one interpolated paint stroke.

9 Scrub between frames 1 and 50.

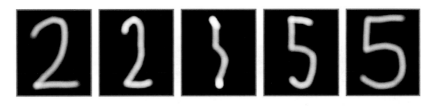

Shake interpolates the *2* and the *5* smoothly from frames 1 to 50.

10 Click the New Canvas icon to remove all strokes from your canvas.

Creating a Write-On Effect

Here's what you have been waiting for—an animated write-on effect.

1 Click the Paint brush icon to return to Paint mode.

2 Make sure that you are in Persist mode for this effect, because you want to animate the stroke over time.

In Persist mode, the paint stroke is active during the entire sequence, as opposed to Frame mode, where the stroke is active only on the current frame.

3 Write the word *Shake* in your neatest handwriting, making sure to form the entire word in one continuous stroke.

Your stroke should look something like this:

OK, I write like a slob. So what!

4   Toggle QuickPaint to Edit mode so that you can see the stroke.

The stroke is now superimposed over the painted letters.

The startPoint and endPoint parameters determine the percentage point at which the stroke starts drawing and the point at which it ends. You can therefore animate a drawn stroke by setting keyframes for the endPoint from 0 to 100 over several frames.

5   In the Edit Controls subtab, turn on the Keyframe toggle for the endPoint parameter at frame 1.

6 Set the value to *0*.

7 Go to frame 50 and set the endPoint to a value of *100*.

8 Drag your slider in the Time Bar.

You should see the word *Shake* animating. Now, make a flipbook to see it moving in real time.

9 In the Globals tab, set the timeRange to *1-50*.

10 Click the Flipbook icon, play the clip, and close when done.

It is a thing of beauty.

Painting in Perspective

Shake allows you to paint in perspective using a Transform CornerPin function in conjunction with QuickPaint.

1 Start by clicking the New Canvas icon.

2 Click the Paint brush icon to enter Paint mode.

3 Select FileIn from the Image tab and go to the Lesson06 folder.

4 FileIn the **wall.0001.tif** clip and fit the image to the Viewer by pressing the F key.

5 Highlight QuickPaint1 and select a CornerPin node from the Transform tab followed by an Over node from the Layer tab.

CornerPin pushes the four corners of an image into four different positions.

6 Connect the output of the **wall** node to the right input of the Over1 node.

Your tree should look like this:

7   Click the right side of the CornerPin1 node to edit its parameters.

8   Adjust the four corners of the CornerPin so that they match the corners of
the building.

The top-right corner of the building isn't visible, so you'll have to zoom
out in the Viewer with the minus sign (−) and pull its upper-right corner
above the upper-right corner of the image. You can use the center line to
judge the accuracy of your placement.

9 Click the right side of QuickPaint1 to edit its parameters.

10 Make sure that you are in Paint mode and that the Frame mode toggle is on.

Frame mode paints only on the current frame.

11 Press the P key to pick color from the wall, and proceed to paint graffiti.

12 Feel free to change the size of the brush as needed in the Paint Controls subtab.

You may have noticed that the profile of your brush has changed and is now a vertical oval. The strokes that you are painting are in perspective with the wall. How about giving the Clone brush a try?

13 Disconnect the **wall** clip from the tree and attach it to the left input of a new QuickPaint node.

14 Double-click the QuickPaint1 node so that you can view and edit it.

15 Select the Clone brush.

The Clone brush will copy from whatever is created by the paint node or whatever comes from the first image input. Shift-drag to move the brush target relative to the source.

16 Shift-drag to offset your paint source.

17 Clone various parts of the image using different brush offsets.

18 While you're at it, experiment with the Smudge brush.

19 Make sure that the Smudge brush is set to the Hard setting when you use it.

20 Return the brush to the Soft setting when you're done.

Dustbusting and Rotoscoping

Dustbusting and rotoscoping are two things you will be doing a lot of, unless of course you have an army of low-paid drones to do it for you. *Dustbusting* is the process of painting out dirt that was introduced onto an image during the film-scanning process. *Rotoscoping* is a frame-by-frame hand-painting technique that is used, for instance, to remove wires and rigs from an image. QuickPaint can help you perform these otherwise thankless jobs.

Dustbusting

When film negative is printed on positive film stock or when film is transferred to video, any small specks of dirt on the surface of the film will also be transferred. Negative dirt appears white when transferred, while dirt on positive film appears black. You just happen to be the sorry sap who will be painting out the dirt.

1 Choose File > New Script and click No when prompted whether to save.

2 FileIn the **surf.1-50.iff** clip from the Lesson06 folder.

3 In the Globals tab, click the Auto button to the right of the timeRange button.

4 Click the Home button at the bottom right of the interface to set the Time Bar range.

5 Click the Flipbook icon.

6 Press the Shift key and drag back and forth to shuttle the flipbook. You can also use the left and right arrow keys to move through the clip frame by frame.

I like the method of rocking and rolling the flipbook using Shift-drag to identify the frames that have dirt.

7 On a piece of paper, use your gnawed-on No. 2 pencil to write down the frames where you can see dirt. If you don't have a pencil and paper, get out of class.

There are a number of frames with both white and black dirt. I see dirt on frames 7, 13, 18, 35, 36, 38, 41, 44, and 50.

8 Close the flipbook.

9 Highlight the **surf** clip and select a QuickPaint node.

10 Make sure that you are in Frame mode.

11 Click the Clone brush.

12 Go to frame 7 and zoom in to the black piece of dirt.

13 Shift-drag to offset your paint source.

Pick any area that is similar in texture and color to the area next to the piece of dirt.

14 Adjust the size of the brush using Control-drag so that the brush is slightly larger than the dirt.

15 Have at it. Paint out the dirt.

16 In the various frames where you find dirt, adjust the Clone offset as needed.

17 Make a flipbook when you think you are done.

If you see more dirt, close the flipbook and continue painting until the clip is clean.

Wire and Rig Removal

Props such as wires and rigs are frequently used to support objects or people in visual effects shots. Of course, they need to be removed later in postproduction. I have provided you with three wire and rig removal shots, presented in order of increasing difficulty.

Wire and Rig Removal No. 1

The first wire and rig removal project includes a clean plate that was shot in production. Assuming that the camera hasn't moved and the lighting conditions are the same for both of the elements, this is the easiest type of rig removal. All you have to do is to paint through to the clean plate.

1 Select File > New Script and click No when prompted whether to save.

2 FileIn **wire1_clean.1-10.iff**, **wire1_final.1-10.iff**, and **wire1.1-10.iff** from the Lesson06 folder.

3 Set the Globals timeRange and Time Bar to *1-10*.

4 Click the Flipbook icon for each clip, starting with **wire1_final**.

The **wire1_final** clip is the finished shot, while the **wire1** clip is the shot you will be painting. It has a large crane and a wire suspending a stunt actor, as well as quite a bit of dirt. The **wire1_clean** clip is a clean plate with no rigging. This shot will be used as a source for the Reveal brush to remove unwanted objects in the frame.

5   Highlight the wire1 clip and select a QuickPaint node.

6   Connect the wire1_clean clip to the second input of QuickPaint1.

7   Click the Reveal brush.

8   Make sure that you are in Persist mode for the first strokes you will be painting.

The crane on the left side of the screen and the stationary car in the foreground need to be painted out of every frame. Because you are in Persist mode, you can paint out these objects on only one frame, and the strokes will be drawn for the entire sequence.

9   Go to frame 10 and paint out the crane and tree on the left side of the screen, the car in the foreground, and the entire cloud area in the sky.

In Persist mode, you will have to paint these areas only once.

10   Set QuickPaint back to Frame mode.

The remaining paint work will be on a frame-by-frame basis.

11   Go to frame 1 and paint out the remainder of the wire connecting the stunt actor.

You might want to zoom in and center on the actor to see the wire more closely. In some cases, you may need to paint over your strokes several times.

12   Continue to paint out the wire on frames 2–10.

13   Make a flipbook of what you have done so far.

Hopefully, the wire and crane are gone and there is no chattering. Chattering is caused by strokes painted in Frame mode that don't completely cover the wire.

But what about the dirt—the small white flecks that appear in different areas of the frame? You will need to remove them using the same process outlined in the previous exercise.

14   Go to each frame that contains dirt and paint it out.

15   Make a flipbook.

If the wires and rigging are gone, the dirt is gone, and there is no chattering, congratulations.

Wire and Rig Removal No. 2

This next wire and rig removal exercise does not include a clean plate, so you will need to clone from various parts of the frame. This is more difficult, because chattering can occur from your paint strokes. The key is to clone from areas that look similar to the area you are painting.

1 Choose File > New Script and click No when prompted whether to save.

2 FileIn **wire2.1-30.iff** and **wire2_final.1-30.iff** from the Lesson06 folder.

3 Set the Globals timeRange and Time Bar to *1-30*.

4 Click the Flipbook icon for each clip, starting with **wire2_final**.

The **wire2_final** clip is an establishing shot for the scene used in the last paint lesson. It is also the finished shot for this exercise. The **wire2** clip is what you will be painting. As in the closer shot, a large crane and wire are suspending a stunt actor, but the moving rig also casts a moving shadow on the adjacent building.

5 Highlight the **wire2** clip and select a QuickPaint node.

6 Make sure that you are in Persist mode.

Once again, in Persist mode, the crane on the left side of the screen is painted out of only one frame, but the strokes will be drawn for the entire sequence.

7   Click the Clone brush.

8   Go to frame 1 and zoom in to the area of the crane.

9   Shift-drag to offset your paint source, and paint out the crane.

Because you are in Persist mode, you will have to paint these areas only once.

10   Change to Frame mode.

The remaining paintwork is all frame-by-frame.

11   Paint out the wire supporting the stunt actor as well as the rig's round shadow on the building.

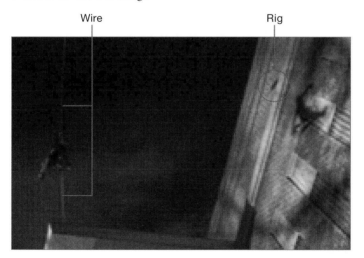

You will need to zoom in to see the wire and rig more closely. In some cases, you may need to paint over your strokes several times.

12 Continue painting on frames 2–30.

13 Make a flipbook when you are done.

Hopefully, the wire and crane are removed with no chattering.

Wire and Rig Removal No. 3

Your third assignment not only lacks a clean plate, but also involves a clip in which the camera is moving. This is one of the most difficult scenarios for a wire removal. You are so screwed. Actually, Shake 4 has a new AutoAlign node, which works great for just this type of shot.

1 Choose File > New Script and click No when prompted whether to save.

2 FileIn **wire3.1-15.iff** and **wire3_final.1-15.iff** from the Lesson06 folder.

3 In the Globals tab, click the Auto button to the right of the timeRange button.

4 Click the Home button at the bottom right of the interface to set the Time Bar range.

5 Click the Flipbook icon for each clip, starting with **wire3_final**.

The **wire3_final** clip is the finished shot, and the **wire3** clip is what you will be painting. With a wire supporting the stunt actor, the camera follows him as he flies across the screen.

The technique I like to use for this type of shot is to create a clean plate and then track it to the motion. Once it is tracked, I can easily paint through to the clean plate to remove any rigs or wires. Prior to Shake 4, this would involve the use of motion trackers.

Enter the AutoAlign node. It is unique among the various transform nodes in that it can combine multiple image inputs into a single output, similar to a layering node. This node is designed to align two or three overlapping images or image sequences in different ways to create a single, seamless output image. Unlike similar photographic tools, the AutoAlign node works with both stills and image sequences. As a result, you could film three side-by-side shots of an expanse of action, and later turn them into a single extremely wide-angle background plate.

In addition, you can align a stationary clean plate with a moving image sequence when you are using images that almost completely overlap. For this exercise, you'll use the AutoAlign node to create a clean plate that does not include the stunt actor or his wire.

6   Highlight the **wire3** clip and select an AutoAlign node from the Transform tab.

To paint the actor out of the image, we need to find another frame where he is clear of his position of frame 1. The last frame, frame 15, will be good.

7   Click FileIn on the Image tab.

8   When the File Browser opens, uncheck the Sequence Listing option.

9   Scroll down to the **wire3.0015.iff** image, choose it, and click OK.

Because there is already a clip named **wire3**, the newly imported clip is called SFileIn1.

10   Rename SFileIn1 *wire3_f15*.

11 Connect wire3_f15 to the middle input of AutoAlign1.

The order of the clips' connection is not important.

12 Double-click AutoAlign1 so that you can view and edit it.

Use the lockedPlate pop-up menu to choose the input to which the clean plate image is connected. Because wire3_f15 will be used to paint out the actor, that is considered the clean plate.

13 Choose Input2 from the lockedPlate pop-up menu.

The analysisRange is automatically set to the duration of the clip, which is 1–15. This is fine.

There are two analysis options—Precise and Robust. In general, set this mode to Precise the first time you analyze the input images. If the results are unsatisfactory, change the mode to Robust, then reanalyze.

14 Leave the mode at the default setting of Precise.

15 Click Analyze.

Shake begins the image analysis. The first frame may take longer than the other frames, but the analysis should speed up after the first frame. As the analysis is performed, the keyframes are set at each analyzed frame.

NOTE ▶ The analysis can be interrupted at any time by pressing Esc.

16 Once the analysis is done, change the blendMode to Mix and scrub through the sequence to see how well the alignment works.

The Mix setting, in the case of two images that almost completely overlap, results in a 50 percent blend of both images. In the above image, the background building appears to align perfectly.

17 In order to use this alignment in QuickPaint, set the following parameters:

▶ Set clipLayer to Input1, so that the moving shot defines the resolution of the output image.

▶ Set lockedPlate to Input1 as well, so that the clean plate image moves along with the background.

▶ Set outputFrame to Input2, and set blendMode to None, so that the only image that is output is the newly animated and aligned clean plate image.

The resulting output image is a transformed version of the wire3_f15 image that matches the position of matching overlapping features in the wire3 image. The auto-aligned wire3_f15 image can now be used to paint.

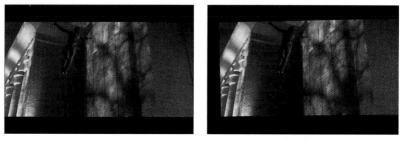

Original wire3 frame 15   Auto-aligned wire3 frame 15

18 Connect the wire3 image to the first input of a QuickPaint node, and the output from the AutoAlign1 node to the second input.

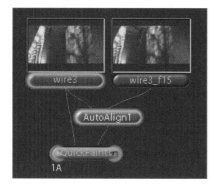

With this setup, you can use the Reveal brush to paint out the stunt actor.

19 Click the Reveal brush.

20 Double-check that you are in Frame mode.

21 Completely paint out the stunt actor.

Congratulations; you have made your first clean plate. The result of the QuickPaint1 node can be rendered so that it can be auto-aligned to the moving sequence.

22 Select a FileOut node on the Image tab.

23 When the File Browser opens, go to your home directory and select the Shake_Output folder that you created in Lesson 2.

24 Enter the filename *wire3_clean.iff* at the bottom of the File Browser and click OK.

25 Right-click the wire3_clean node and choose Render > Render FileOut Nodes from the pop-up menu.

26 In the Render Parameters window, set the timeRange to 1 and click Render.

The Monitor window appears and shows the progress of your render. When it completes, FileIn the wire_clean.0001.iff image.

27 Click FileIn, and when the File Browser opens, uncheck the Sequence Listing option.

> **NOTE ▶** It is important that you uncheck the Sequence Listing option, because single-frame clips imported in this way have an infinite length. A single-frame clip is being imported, and we want it to be visible over the entire length of the sequence.

28 Scroll down to the wire3_clean.0001.iff image, choose it, and click OK.

The cleanplate image can now be auto-aligned to the moving sequence and will become the paint source to remove the wire.

29 Rename SFileIn1 *cleanplate*.

30 Create a new AutoAlign node.

31 Connect wire3 to the left input and cleanplate to the middle input.

32 Double-click AutoAlign2 so that you can view and edit it.

Use the lockedPlate pop-up menu to connect the cleanplate image to its input.

33 Choose Input2 from the lockedPlate pop-up menu.

34 Click Analyze.

35 Once the analysis is done, change the blendMode to Mix and scrub through the sequence to see how well the alignment works.

36 To prepare the clip for painting, set both clipLayer and lockedPlate to Input1, set outputFrame to Input2, and set the blendMode to None.

The cleanplate now matches the motion of the **wire3** clip.

37 Connect the wire3 image to the first input of a new QuickPaint node, and the output from the AutoAlign2 node to the second input.

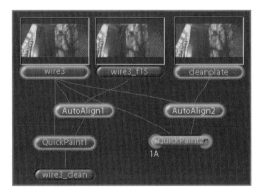

38 Click the Reveal brush.

39 Make sure that you are in Frame mode.

40 Zoom in to the area above the stunt actor, and completely paint out the wires attached to him on every frame.

Wire

Black will appear in some frames when you are painting with the Reveal brush. This is a result of the AutoAlign process. On any frames where black appears at the top of the frame, you will need to use the Clone brush to repair those areas.

41 Switch to the Clone brush as necessary to fix any black areas painted through from the AutoAligned paint source.

42 Make a flipbook once you think you've got it.

43 Quit Shake.

Dustbusting and wire and rig removal can now be added to your repertoire of rapidly increasing Shake skills.

Lesson Review

1. Which stroke mode allows you to keep the stroke over the course of all of your frames?

2. What is dustbusting?

3. What is rotoscoping?

4. What is the difference between the Reveal brush and the Clone brush?

5. When would you use the AutoAlign node?

Answers

1. Persist mode.

2. Dustbusting is the process of painting over dirt on an image.

3. Rotoscoping is a frame-by-frame hand-painting technique to create imagery over time.

4. The Reveal brush exposes whatever is in the second image input; the Clone brush copies from whatever is created by the paint node or whatever comes from the first image input.

5. Use the AutoAlign node to easily align a stationary clean plate with a moving image sequence.

Keyboard Shortcuts

Paint

P	picks color
Z	makes a magnetic drag in Edit mode
Control-drag	sets the brush size
Shift-drag	offsets the paint clone source

7

Lesson **7**
Tracking

Tracking is a technique that involves selecting a particular region of an image and analyzing its motion over time. Once analyzed, the motion can be applied to another clip.

In this lesson you will use tracking to stabilize shaky images, match-move a neon globe to the top of a building, and perform a four-point track to insert an image onto a television screen.

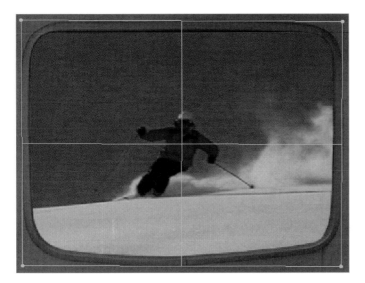

You will use corner-pinning to match the perspective of the skier to that of the TV screen after they are composited together and tracked.

One-Point Tracking with MatchMove

Shake has three tracking nodes: Tracker, Stabilize, and MatchMove. Tracker is a generic generator of an unlimited number of curves and is useful for passing these curves to the transform nodes. Stabilize removes bounce or jitter from a clip and can generate up to four trackers to be used for positioning, scaling, and rotational stabilizing. MatchMove can track up to four points and apply the tracked motion from one clip to another.

Despite all the demos you love to see, tracking is rarely a magic bullet that works on the first attempt. In the MatchMove exercise, I'll provide you with some strategies to help you get accurate tracks.

View the Clips

It is always best to view the clips that you'll be tracking. It will help you choose the proper feature to track.

1   Open Shake.

2   FileIn the **building.1-50.iff**, **building_comp.1-50.iff**, and **neon_globe.1-50.iff** clips from the Lesson07 folder.

3   Start by setting the Global timeRange to *1-50*.

4   While you're at it, click the Home icon at the bottom right of the screen to make the Time Bar's low and high values match those of the Globals timeRange.

5   Make a flipbook of `building_comp`.

The globe was tracked and composited on top of the building.

6   Make a flipbook of your two elements: `building` and `neon_globe`.

You will be motion-tracking the `building` clip and applying that motion to the `neon_globe` clip.

7   Close all your flipbooks when you're done.

Tracking Workflow

Here is your basic tracking workflow:

▶   Play through your clip several times to determine a good track point.

▶   Attach your tracking MatchMove node to the clip.

▶   Make sure the onscreen controls are visible in the Viewer.

- ▶ Go to the frame where you want to start tracking.

- ▶ Position the tracker at the point you want to track, and adjust the reference pattern and the search region.

- ▶ Click either the reverse or forward tracking button.

Positioning the Tracker

By default, the tracker appears in the Viewer. Each tracker has a reference pattern, search region, and track point.

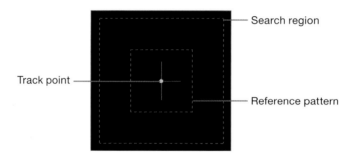

- ▶ Reference pattern—The inner box is the reference pattern. It defines a small pattern that the tracker will search for in subsequent frames. It's always a good idea to choose a region with good contrast and detail. A corner with sharp contrast is usually a good area to track, because motion can be detected easily in any direction. The reference pattern can be scaled to the desired size.

- ▶ Search region—The outer box is the search region, which should be the maximum amount your track point will move between frames. The larger it is, the slower the tracker is. The search region can be sized in the same fashion as the reference pattern.

- ▶ Track point—The crosshairs constitute the track point, which represents the position of the motion track. Normally, the track point is at the center of the tracker, but it can be offset if the reference pattern becomes obscured.

Pick a Good Reference Pattern

The ideal reference pattern is one that doesn't change perspective, scale, or rotation, and does not go offscreen or get obscured by other objects. It also doesn't change overall brightness or color, has a very high contrast, and is distinct from other patterns in the same neighborhood. Meanwhile, in the real world, you have to contend with all of these factors, which will cause your trackers to lose accuracy. A successful composite requires an accurate track.

1   Make sure that you are positioned at frame 1 of the timeline.

2   Go to the Transform tab, right-click MatchMove, and choose Create.

3   Connect the output of the **building** clip to the right input (background input) of MatchMove1.

4   Position the tracker over the 12 o'clock position.

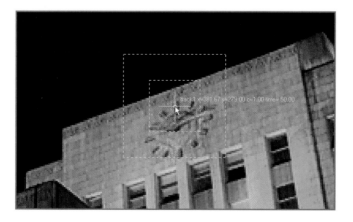

You might want to zoom in to allow precise placement of the tracker.

5   Size the reference pattern so that it has only a few pixels around 12 o'clock.

Pick a Good Search Region

You should position and size your search region to match both the movement and the patterns near your reference pattern. Set it to the maximum amount that your track point will move between frames. The larger it is, the slower the tracker will be.

1   Size the search region around the outside of the reference pattern.

How do you know if the search region is the right size? If you make the search region too small, the tracker will lose the reference pattern. If it's unnecessarily large, it will take too long to process. The key is to make the search region as small as possible without getting tracking errors.

Track the Image in Its Highest Quality

▶   Ideally, you should be tracking an image with the greatest amount of raw data, so make sure both proxyScale and proxyRatio settings are turned off. Once the tracks are done, return to your proxy settings.

▶   In some cases, you may in fact want to modify your images to improve contrast in the reference pattern, either with a ContrastLum or ContrastRGB. Since you are just using this image to generate tracks, you are not obliged to keep the contrast-modified image for the rest of your composite.

▶   Finally, you may sometimes have problems when random film grain is too severe and your reference pattern becomes useless. To reduce the effects of grain, click the preProcess button in the tracker before you track.

Creating a Tracking Curve

When creating a tracking curve, you'll need to make sure that the trackRange, matchSpace, and subPixelResolution parameters are set properly and that you know how the Track buttons work.

▶   trackRange—When you create a tracking node, the length of the input clip is automatically fed into the trackRange parameter of the tracker. The tracker will run from the current frame to either the beginning or end of the range, since you can track forward or backward. In this case, the trackRange is 1–50.

▶   matchSpace—The tracker works best with a high-contrast reference pattern. The human eye sees contrast as represented by value. However, you may sometimes have an image with higher contrast in saturation or hue. Also, when attempting to track a pattern, pixels are matched according to the correlation between the selected color space: either luminance, hue, or saturation. By default, luminance is selected, and that will work well here because you are tracking an illuminated clock. To switch to a different color space, just click the + next to Tolerances to reveal the matchSpace parameters.

A shot's contrast may also be higher in one specific RGB channel than in others; for example, the blue channel might have a wider range than the red or green channels. In that case, you could put a Reorder node (from the Color tab) with the channels set to bbb on the image, and then track with luminance as your matchSpace.

▶ subPixelResolution—The precision (and therefore the time) of your track is determined by subPixelResolution, which by default is 1/64. For this track, 1/64 is fine; for more precise tracks, change the value.

▶ Track buttons—The Track buttons are located under the Viewer when your tracking node is loaded into the Parameters workspace. The Track buttons start the tracking, going either backward or forward in time from the current frame. For this reason, you generally are positioning the tracker on frame 1 when you start. The tracker will go for the entire time specified in the trackRange parameter.

Track the Building
Enough talking already; it's time for some tracking.

1 Turn on limitProcessing in the MatchMove1 node.

This will speed up processing. You'll see what I mean in a moment.

2   Click the forward tracking button.

When limitProcessing is turned on, the screen turns black except for the area enclosed within the search region. This will create a domain of definition (DOD) around the bounding box of all active trackers. Only that portion of the image will be loaded from disk when tracking; therefore, tracking goes more quickly. This has no effect on the final output image.

MatchMove tracks each frame of the **building** clip and superimposes the tracked points for each frame.

NOTE ▶ To stop the tracker at any time, press Esc.

Now that you have acquired the tracking data, you can apply it to another clip.

Apply a Tracking Curve

In this case, the default settings in MatchMove for applying the curve are already set the way you want, with the exception of applyTransform. Remember, there are always exceptions. For different types of match-moving, you may want to change some of these settings:

▶ trackType—Allows you to choose what track type you want, either one-point(panning), which is the default; two-point (panning, scaling, and/or rotation); or four-point (corner-pinning).

▶ applyX/applyY—For panning, you can select applyX or applyY separately, or you can select both. Both are on by default. applyScale and applyRotate will show up in the menu only if 2 pt is selected.

▶ applyTransform—The applyTransform function applies the transform needed to stabilize the image. It is inactive by default. You will need to turn it on for this project.

Now let's apply the tracking curve.

1   Connect the output of the neon_globe node to the foreground or first input of MatchMove1.

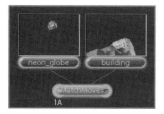

2   In the outputType pop-up box, choose IAdd.

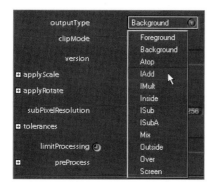

This selects the method by which you will combine the foreground with the background.

3   Make sure that 1 pt is selected as the trackType.

4   Turn on applyTransform.

The tracking data is now applied to the **neon_globe** clip.

5   Drag the Time Bar to various frames.

The globe's motion is now following the motion of the **building** clip. It's not in the right position, but it is tracked.

6   Go to frame 1, highlight the **neon_globe** clip, and select Move2D from the Transform tab.

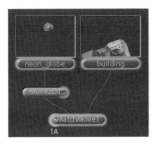

7   Reposition the neon_globe with Move_2D1 so that it rests on the top of the building.

8   Double-click MatchMove1 and click the Flipbook icon under the Viewer
to test the results of your track.

The track looks pretty good, but what if your reference pattern becomes
obscured at some point?

Offset Tracking

Sometimes your original reference pattern gets obscured. In those instances,
you can offset the search region from the track point. You will simulate this
with a new track and the **building** clip.

1   Turn off applyTransform so that MatchMove1 is not trying to move the
foreground at the same time you are trying to track.

2   Set the outputType pop-up to Background so that the foreground is not
composited with the background.

3 Scroll down the Parameters workspace, turn off the Visibility of track1, and turn on the Visibility of track2.

4 Go to frame 50.

Just for fun, you will track track2 backward.

5 Position track2 over the 6 o'clock position of the clock, and size the reference pattern and search region the way you did for track1.

6 Click the reverse tracking button and press the Esc key at about frame 25 to stop the track.

7 Drag the Time Bar to frame 25 if you are not already there.

The track point at frame 25 just became obscured. You're pretending, remember. If you turn on the Offset Track function, the search region and reference pattern can be moved to a new location while keeping the track point in the same location.

▶ Offset Track Off—The track search region/reference pattern and the track point are linked. If you move one, the other follows.

▶ Offset Track On—The search region/reference pattern and the track point are offset from each other.

8 Turn on offset tracking.

Make sure to turn on offset tracking before you move the search region.

9 Position track2's search region and reference pattern over the 11 o'clock position.

10 Click the reverse tracking button to continue tracking.

The track point follows the same path, but the new search region is used to acquire the tracking data.

Averaging Tracks

A common technique is to track forward from the first frame to the last, and then create a second track, tracking backward from the last frame to the first. It just so happens that you have already done this. What a coincidence! These two tracks are then averaged together to hopefully derive a more accurate track. Because MatchMove always uses track1 for *x-y* transformations, you will need to copy track1 to a different track before averaging.

1   At the bottom of the Parameters workspace, right-click track3 and choose Load Track.

2   When the Select Track window opens, choose MatchMove1.track1 from the pop-up menu and click OK.

This loads track1 into track3.

3   Right-click track1 and choose Average Tracks.

A window opens that lets you average up to four input trackers.

4   Choose MatchMove1.track2 and MatchMove1.track3 from the first two pop-up menus, and leave the last two pop-ups at None. Click OK when you're done.

This creates an expression in both the track1X and track1Y parameters. The expression for the track1X parameter looks like this:

```
(MatchMove1.track3X + MatchMove1.track2X) / 2
```

You can see the effect of this averaging clearly in the Curve Editor.

5   Expand the track1Name, track2Name, and track3Name parameter groups, and click the clock icon next to the trackX parameter for each track.

6 Select the Curve Editor in the tool tabs.

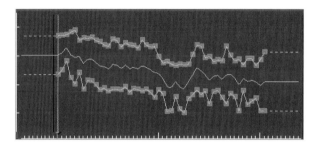

The middle curve represents the averaged track1. Slight differences in the tracks have been averaged, yielding a more accurate result. Let's take a look.

7 Choose IAdd from the outputType pop-up box.

8 Turn on applyTransform.

9 Click the Flipbook icon, and play the clip when it's done loading.

You should have a pretty decent track at this point.

One-Point Tracking with Stabilization

Stabilization involves selecting a particular region of an image and analyzing its motion over time. Once analyzed, the motion data is inverted and applied to the clip, causing it to become stable. Clips need to be stabilized for a variety of reasons, such as a shaky camera move or weaving created by an unsteady camera gate.

This exercise involves stabilizing a clip of an extreme telephoto shot of a NASA space shuttle separating from its fuel tanks. You will use both the Stabilize and SmoothCam nodes to accomplish the task.

Tracking with a Stabilize Node

1   Choose File > New Script and click No when prompted whether to save.

2   FileIn the **separation.1-70.iff** clip from the Lesson07 folder.

3   Press the F key to see the entire image in the Viewer.

4   Set the Globals timeRange to *1-70,* and click the Home button at the bottom right of the screen to make the Time Bar match that duration.

5   Make a flipbook.

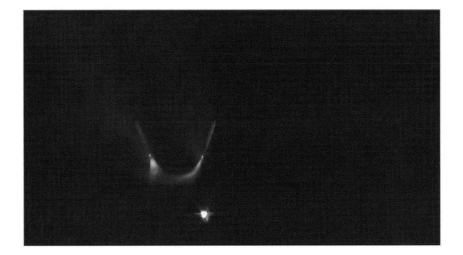

A one-point track is needed to stabilize the camera motion.

6 Attach a Stabilize node from the Transform tab to the **separation** clip.

Stabilize is a dedicated tracking node that locks down an image, removing problems such as camera shake or gate weave. You can do one-point (position), two-point (position, scaling, or rotation), or four-point (corner-pinning) stabilization.

7 Position the tracker over the space shuttle's engine.

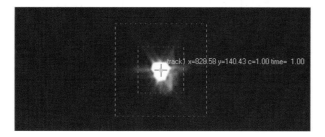

8 Turn on limitProcessing to speed up the tracking analysis.

9 Click the forward tracking button.

With limitProcessing on, the screen turns black except for the area around the four tracks, and the space shuttle's motion is analyzed.

10 Turn on applyTransform.

11 Right-click the Flipbook icon to open the Render Parameters window.

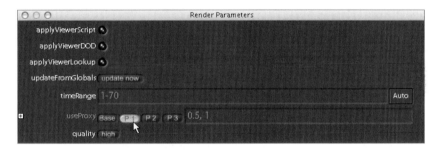

12 Click P1 in the useProxy section, and then click Render.

This will create a flipbook at half resolution. The space shuttle is stabilized, but notice how a black border is created around the image as a result of the stabilization. This can be fixed by cropping the image.

13 Close the flipbook.

14 Add a Window node from the Transform tab after Stabilize1.

Window is exactly like a crop, but you enter the lower-left corner, and then the x and y resolution.

15 Set the Res parameter to 960x540 and drag the cropLeft and cropBottom
sliders so that the image is centered as shown below.

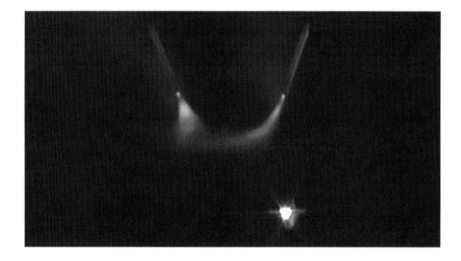

16 Right-click the Flipbook icon again to open the Render Parameters
window.

17 Click Base in the useProxy section to disable the use of proxies, and then
click Render.

The space shuttle is stabilized and the black border is gone. Woo-hoo!

18 Close the flipbook.

Tracking with a SmoothCam Node
The SmoothCam node differs from the other tracking nodes in that it doesn't
focus the track on a small group of pixels. Instead, it evaluates the entire image at
once, using advanced motion-analysis techniques to extract transformation data.

Once this information is derived, the node has two modes. It can smooth the
shot, eliminating unwanted jitter while maintaining the general motion of the
camera, or it can lock the shot, stabilizing the subject. SmoothCam can affect
translation, rotation, zoom, and perspective, making it more flexible for certain operations than the other tracking nodes.

The SmoothCam node is primarily useful for removing unwanted trembling from less-than-stable crane or jib arm moves, eliminating teetering from hand-held walking shots, or reducing vibrations in vehicle shots. The SmoothCam node can also be used to stabilize shots that might be difficult to lock using the Stabilize node.

1   Click the Stabilize1 node to select it.

2   Right-click SmoothCam on the Transform tab and choose Replace from the pop-up menu.

3   Choose an analysisQuality mode. Start with Normal, which provides excellent results in most cases.

   NOTE ▸ If, at the end of this process, the result is not what you'd hoped, then try again with the analysisQuality mode set to High. Be aware this will significantly increase the time it takes to perform the analysis.

4   Click the Analyze button.

   Time to take a break and go annoy somebody, because SmoothCam takes a while to analyze.

5   Once the analysis has concluded, set steadyMode to Lock.

For images with high-frequency vibration, like an image shot from a helicopter, you could use the Smooth parameter to remove the jitter, while retaining the overall camera movement.

6   Go to frame 1 and click the right side of the Window1 node.

7   Drag the cropLeft and cropBottom sliders to center the image.

8   Click the Flipbook icon.

SmoothCam stabilized the space shuttle image just as effectively as the Stabilize node did. The processing took longer using SmoothCam, but it required far less work.

9   Close the flipbook and get ready for some four-point tracking.

Applying Four-Point Tracking

Four-point tracking is traditionally used to match the perspective of one shot and apply it to another—for instance, tracking the four corners of a sign and replacing it with a new billboard. In this example, you will track a television screen and insert an image inside it.

For this exercise, you will use Stabilize instead of MatchMove. This has several advantages:

▶   More flexibility in what extra nodes you can apply, because you separate the composite out of MatchMove.

▶   Better control over the transform concatenation of the foreground.

▶   Better control over the premultiplication of the foreground.

▶   Accurate pass-through of onscreen controls.

▶   Intuitive control of foreground positioning.

Workflow for Match-Moving with Stabilize

Here is the workflow for match-moving with a Stabilize node:

▶   Attach Stabilize to the node you are going to be tracking and generate your tracks—in this example, the TV.

▶ Extract the Stabilize node (select it and press the E key), and reattach it to the image you want to transform—in this example, the skier.

▶ Turn on the transformation with applyTransform and change Stabilize to match.

▶ Composite the Stabilize node over the background with an Over node.

▶ Insert a Viewport node above the Stabilize node to adjust the frame around what you want to track.

▶ Insert a CornerPin between the Viewport node and the Stabilize node. This is used to match the foreground clip's perspective and size to the background image.

Viewing the Elements

OK, let's see what we're about to create.

1 Choose File > New Script and click No when prompted whether to save.

2 FileIn the **tv_comp.1-70.iff**, **tv.1-70.iff,** and **ski_powder.1-70.iff** clips from the Lesson07 folder.

3 Set the Globals timeRange and Time Bar to *1-70*.

4 Make a flipbook of the **tv_comp** clip.

A four-point track was used to match the perspective of the TV screen and to place the skier inside.

5   Make a flipbook of your two sequences: **tv** and `ski_powder`.

The TV screen clip has four points on it, obviously placed by a visual effects supervisor who cares. This will make tracking relatively painless. The skier clip is a great action shot that will be used for the foreground insert.

6   Close your flipbooks.

Track the TV Screen

Start by tracking the TV screen with a Stabilize node.

1   Highlight the **tv** clip and select a Stabilize node from the Transform tab.

At frame 1 of the sequence, you will place four tracks starting at the lower-left corner and moving counterclockwise.

2   Go to frame 1 of the sequence.

3   Place track1 over the lower-left + of the TV screen.

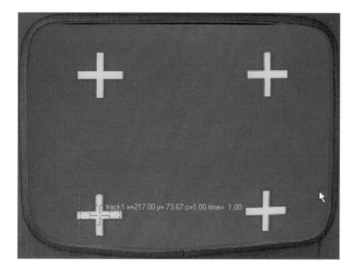

4   Set the subPixelResolution to 1/256.

Because you need to make sure the elements fit together seamlessly, a
more precise setting than 1/64 is used.

5   Turn on the visibility for track2 through track4 at the bottom of the
Parameters workspace.

6 Place track2 on the lower-right +, track3 on the upper-right +, and track4 on the upper-left +.

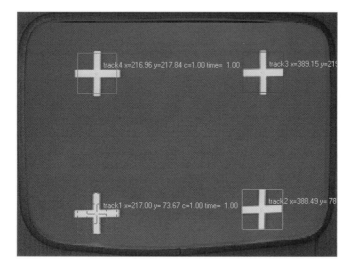

7 Turn on limitProcessing, which will make the tracking analysis go faster.

8 Click the forward tracking button.

Because limitProcessing is active, the screen turns black except for the area around the four tracks.

Creating the Composite

Since the TV was shot as a blue screen, you would think that a matte process would be used to composite the skier into the TV. Normally, you would use what is known as a *keyer* to cut out the blue portion of the screen and replace it with a different image. In this case, the blue screen blows, and you would put yourself into a spot of bother if you tried using one. Second, the keying lesson is later in this book, and that would require my changing the order of my lessons, and that would put *me* into a spot of bother. So when you have a blue screen that won't key, it is best to use a rotoshape.

1   Go back to frame 1.

2   Add a RotoShape node from the Image tab.

3   Click the left side of the **tv** clip to view it.

4   Set the Res parameters in the RotoShape node to 720x308.

   This sets the resolution to match the TV.

5   Draw a shape just inside the perimeter of the TV screen.

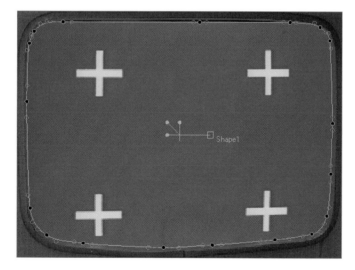

The blue spill around the edges of the screen will eventually need to be removed. Now is as good a time as any.

6   Double-click the **tv** clip and select HueCurves from the Color tab.

HueCurves allows you to perform various color corrections on isolated hues through the use of the Curve Editor. Typically, this tool is used for spill suppression.

7   Find the hue of the area you want to color-correct by using the Color Picker. Click the Color Picker tab in the Node View.

8   Drag over the blue color in the TV screen to sample the color.

9   In the Color Picker, scroll down and expand the Values parameter.

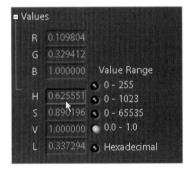

10   Note that the Hue value is 0.62.

You will use this value when suppressing the blue in the HueCurves.

11 Expand the Parameters workspace so that you can see the HueCurve parameters and the Curve Editor.

12 Drag the vertical scroll bar to the right of the parameters until you can see bSuppress.

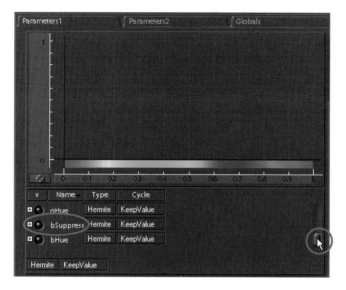

13 Activate bSuppress.

14 Drag the knot nearest 0.6 in the Curve Editor down as close as possible to 0.

The saturation is decreased in that particular hue, turning the pure blues to gray.

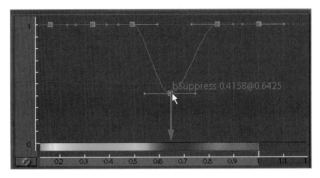

15 At the bottom of the Curve Editor, change Key to *0.62*, the value you sampled in the Color Picker, and Value to *0*.

The blue spill is gone, and you now have the necessary elements to create the composite using a KeyMix function. More on KeyMix in a moment.

16 Switch from the Color Picker tab to the Node View tab.

17 With the pointer over the Node workspace, select the Stabilize1 node and press the E key to extract it.

18 Connect the **ski_powder** clip to the Stabilize1 node.

19 Highlight the HueCurves1 node and select a KeyMix node from the Layer tab.

The KeyMix function mixes two images together through the specified channel of a third image. The order of connection from left to right is background, foreground, and key or matte.

20 Connect Stabilize1 to the middle input, and connect RotoShape1 to the right input.

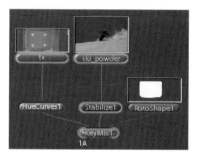

21 Set KeyMix1's clipMode to Foreground so that the resolution of the composite matches that of the **tv** clip.

Applying the Tracking Data

The skier is composited into the TV screen, but the tracking data needs to be activated in the Stabilize node.

1 Click the right side of Stabilize1 to edit its parameters.

2 In Stabilize1, set applyTransform to Active, set inverseTransform to Match, and select 4 pt for the trackType.

3 Drag through the Time Bar.

What is wrong with this picture? To start, the shape that you drew doesn't follow the motion of the TV. The rotoshape needs the tracking data applied to it as well. In addition, the skier's size and position are wrong.

4   Highlight the RotoShape1 node and select another Stabilize node from the Transform tab.

5   Turn on the visibility for track2 through track4 at the bottom of the Parameters workspace.

6   Right-click track1 and choose Load Track.

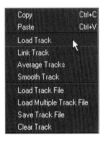

7   In the Select Track window, choose Stabilize1.track1 from the pop-up menu, and then click OK.

Stabilize1.track1 is loaded into Stabilize2.track1.

8   Using the same method, load Stabilize1.track2-4 into Stabilize2.track2-4.

9   Make applyTransform active, set inverseTransform to Match, and select 4 pt for the trackType.

NOTE ▶ For those of you using the full version of Shake, you could have just copied and pasted the Stabilize1 node using Command-C and Command-V. The trial version included with this book does not allow you to copy and paste, hence the hoops you must jump through.

To position and size the skier, you will use a Viewport node and a CornerPin node.

10 Go back to frame 1.

11 Highlight the `ski_powder` clip and select a Viewport node from the Transform tab.

Viewport is like a crop, but it keeps the image information outside the frame so that you can do transformations afterward. Using a Viewport will help you to better place the `ski_powder` clip in conjunction with the CornerPin node that will be added in a moment.

12 View and edit Viewport1.

13 Adjust the outline of the Viewport1 node so that the crosshairs are in the center of the skier's chest.

14 Add a CornerPin node after Viewport1, and click the left side of KeyMix1 to view the composite.

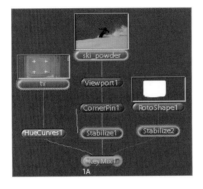

15 Place the four corners of the CornerPin around the screen to form a rectangle, using the horizontal and vertical lines outside the TV screen to guide you. Changing the points in the Viewer will change the x0, y0 through x3, y3 parameter values.

The CornerPin node puts the skier into the same perspective as the TV.

NOTE ▸ Dragging halfway between the points of the CornerPin on the top, bottom, left, and right sides offsets the points but keeps them in proper perspective.

16 Click the Flipbook icon to see what you've done so far.

The shot seems to be tracked pretty well. So get ready for the final touches.

17 Close the flipbook when you are finished viewing.

Treating the Skier

The composite is progressing nicely, but the image in the TV could use some scan lines and color correction.

1 Add a Mult node after Stabilize1.

Color-correct the skier to be a bit darker and bluer.

2 Adjust the R, G, B values so that the image is darker and bluer. I used the following values: R = 0.7, G = 0.8, and B = 1.2.

To add a poor man's version of television scan lines, we'll improvise by subtracting lines created with the Checker node.

3 Click the Checker button on the Image tab.

Checker generates a checkerboard within the width and height of the image.

4 Set the Res parameters to 720x308 to match the resolution of the **tv** clip.

5 Click the Home button below the Viewer to make sure that you are view-ing at a zoom ratio of 1:1.

An odd zoom ratio can affect the appearance of the lines.

6   Change the Size to *100* and *0*.

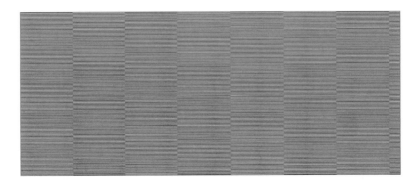

Lines, lines, and more lines …

7   Insert ISub from the Layer tab after Mult1, and connect Checker1 to the right input.

ISub subtracts one image from another and works well to achieve the scan line effect.

8   Click the left side of KeyMix1 to view the composite.

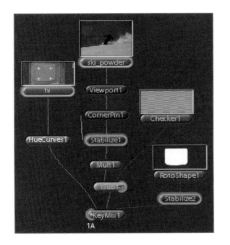

The lines are way too heavy, so let's mix them out a bit.

9   Change the percent setting to 5.

10 Make another flipbook.

To polish this, it would be nice to add some screen reflection around the edges.

11 Close the flipbook.

Adding Reflection

Screen reflection can be added around the edges of the TV by using another rotoshape and an IAdd node.

1   Click RotoShape on the Image tab and set the Res parameters to 720x308.

2   Click the left side of the **tv** clip to view it.

3   Go to frame 1 and draw a shape around the outside edge of the screen.

Your shape should look like this:

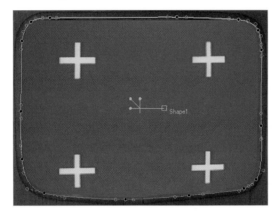

The tracking data must also be applied to this new RotoShape node.

4   If you have the full version of Shake, copy and paste the Stabilize1 node and connect the RotoShape2 node to it.

If you are using the trial version of Shake, do the following:

▶   Highlight the RotoShape2 node and select another Stabilize node from the Transform tab.

▶   Turn on the visibility for track2 through track4 at the bottom of the Parameters workspace.

▶   Right-click track1 and choose Load Track.

▶   In the Select Track window, choose Stabilize1.track1 from the pop-up menu and click OK.

▶   Using the same method, load Stabilize1.track2-4 into Stabilize3.track2-4.

▶   Make applyTransform active, set inverseTransform to Match, and select 4 pt for the trackType.

To generate the edge matte that is needed to create the reflection, subtract RotoShape1 from RotoShape2.

5 Add an ISub node from the Layer tab after Stabilize3, and connect
Stabilize2 to the right input.

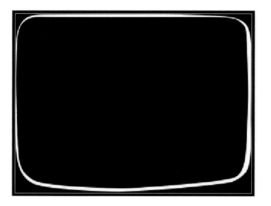

This creates an edge matte that is the difference between the two shapes.

6 Select HueCurves1 and add an IAdd node from the Layer tab.

IAdd adds one image to another and will create our reflection.

7 Connect Mult1 to the second input of IAdd1, and connect ISub2 to the
Mask input.

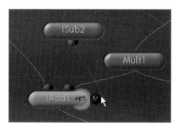

Plugging in to the mask input ensures that the reflection will be added
only in the areas defined by the edge matte.

8 Click the left side of KeyMix1 to view it, and click the right side of IAdd1 to edit it.

Your tree should look like this:

9 Set the clipMode to Foreground and adjust the slider so that you can see what the IAdd is doing. Set the percentage to *10* when you are done fiddling with it.

10 Make a flipbook.

Now *that* is how you do a four-point track.

11 Quit Shake.

Making Tracker Adjustments

If the tracker misses, which it never does, you have a few options:

▶ Stop the tracker, go to the bad frame, reposition the crosshairs, and click the tracking button again. You don't need to go back to your start frame. Frames that are outside the tolerance (see below) are marked in red on the Time Bar.

▶ Activate the preProcess option in the tracker. This applies a small blur to the footage and reduces irregularities due to film grain.

▶ Lower your referenceTolerance value, and track again from the beginning or from the frame before the bad frames. The lower the referenceTolerance is, the more forgiving the tracker will be—but it will also be less accurate. Access the referenceTolerance parameter by clicking the + next to the Tolerances parameter group in your tracking node.

▶ Start over, and switch referenceBehavior, located in the tolerances parameter group, from "use start frame" to "update every frame." This means that instead of trying to compare the tracking region with the first "pure" frame, the tracking algorithm will try to match to the previous frame. If you retrack from the middle of a sequence, it will consider your new start frame as your reference frame with either setting.

▶ At any time, you can turn on the AutoKey button in the Viewer and manually adjust a track point by simply grabbing it and putting it where you need it. You can use the + and – keys by the Backspace key to zoom in and out to see the points more easily.

▶ Change the matchSpace from luminance to hue or saturation, and then retrack. The matchSpace parameter determines which image value the tracking algorithm will be using. The matchSpace controls are in the Tolerances parameter group of your tracking node. Just click the + next to Tolerances to reveal the matchSpace parameters.

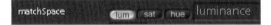

▶ Change the subPixelResolution to get more precise tracks. The tracker will take longer, but it will be more accurate.

NOTE ▶ When checking the accuracy of your tracks, it's best to turn off applyTransform to see whether the curves are matching up to the points.

▶ Another technique you can use to assist with difficult shots is to insert tracking keyframes manually. For example, if you have 100 frames to track, you can put in a keyframe every 5 or 10 frames with the AutoKey feature. A helpful trick is to set an increment of 5 or 10 in the Time Bar and press the left arrow or right arrow to jump by the increment amount and set keyframes. Once your keyframes are entered, return to frame 1 and set the failureBehavior under the Tolerances submenu to "use existing key to predict location." The tracker searches along the preexisting motion path to find matching patterns.

Lesson Review

1. How many tracking nodes does Shake have, and what are they?
2. What is a reference pattern? What is a search region?
3. How do you combine multiple tracks?
4. What does offset tracking do, and when is it appropriate to use it?
5. What is the difference between the Stabilize and SmoothCam nodes?
6. What is HueCurves used for?

Answers

1. Shake has three tracking nodes: Tracker, Stabilize, and MatchMove.
2. A reference pattern defines a small pattern that will be searched for in subsequent frames when tracking; the search region is the maximum amount your track point will move between frames.
3. Use the Average Tracks function to combine multiple tracks.
4. Offset tracking is used when your reference pattern becomes obscured. In this mode, the track point follows the same path, but a new search region or reference pattern is used to acquire the tracking data.
5. The SmoothCam node is an alternative to the Stabilize node for stabilizing images and is more automated.
6. HueCurves is a process that effectively removes a particular color from an image.

8

Lesson Files	APTS_Shake > Lessons > Lesson08
Media	bullet.1-19.iff
	bullet_comp.1-19.iff
	glass.1-19.cin
	reflection.1-19.iff
Time	This lesson takes approximately 1 hour to complete.
Goals	Create proxies, proxies, and more proxies
	Integrate Kodak Cineon 10-bit log images into a composite
	Create a composite at low resolution and then convert to high resolution

Lesson 8
Film Compositing

In this lesson, you will create a film composite using low-resolution proxies to work faster and more efficiently. Once you're happy with the composite, you will switch over and work with the original high-resolution film images.

This is the composite you will build in this lesson.

Film Resolution Files

Film resolution files are generally scanned at a size of 2048x1556 pixels, but practically speaking, effects artists work with a variety of different film image sizes. The large size of film images means longer processing and slower interaction. It also means that you can charge more for the job. Sweet.

1   Open Shake.

2   FileIn the **glass.1-19.cin** sequence from the Lesson08 folder.

3   Click the Fit Image to Viewer icon in the Viewer.

4   Click frame 5 on the Time Bar.

Patience. It will take a moment to update. The **glass** clip is an 1828x988-pixel Kodak 10-bit Cineon log clip. In the title bar of the Viewer, it says that the clip is 16-bit RGB. Shake takes the 10-bit log clip and blows it out to 16 bits. It is still in log space and as a result looks washed out, because Cineon files are flattened, or compressed, in the highlights and shadows.

5   Switch the Viewer to Scrolling Update mode.

This displays each line, starting from the bottom, as the image renders. This mode is good for slower renders.

6   Advance the Time Bar by 1 frame.

Working with film resolution files is definitely slower than working with the clips you have seen so far. They take longer to load and longer to process. Shake has a number of tools—namely, proxies—to speed up interaction when working with these larger files.

Proxies

A *proxy* is a lower-resolution image that you substitute for a high-resolution image so you can work faster. Think of proxies as the Mini Me of visual effects. Because the images are smaller, you drastically decrease your disk access time, your memory consumption, and your processing time. Naturally, your quality will suffer as well, which is why proxies are generally for testing purposes. Once you are done assembling your script with proxies, you return your script to full resolution to render your final output.

In this example, you have the full-resolution image and a ⅓ proxy. In the following images, you can see that the proxy takes up one-ninth of the space, meaning potentially only 11 percent of the processing time, memory usage, and disk activity.

Shake will automatically adjust pixel-based values to compensate for the lower resolution, so a Pan of 100 pixels is calculated to be only 33.333 pixels when using a ⅓ proxy. The actual Pan parameters in the interactive text field will not be modified.

There are three basic approaches for using proxies. These are controlled in the Globals tab of the Parameters workspace.

▶ useProxy—You want to speed up your processing, but you don't plan on working on the project for an extended period of time.

▶ useProxy and pre-render your proxy files—You are working on a project for a long time, the project is extremely large, and your high-resolution files are probably on a remote disk. You will be doing many flipbook tests.

▶ interactiveScale—Your general speed is fine, but you want to adjust nodes quickly and interactively at full resolution. This will not affect your flip-books or renders.

Creating On-the-Fly Proxies

On-the-fly proxies are generated only when needed and are discarded when your disk cache is full. The disk cache is a temporary storage area on your disk, which Shake uses to improve system performance. The Globals useProxy parameter reads your input images and scales them down, placing them first into memory and then into the disk cache as memory runs out. It then recomputes the script at the lower values and leaves it at that resolution until you return it to full resolution.

NOTE ▶ The useProxy setting will affect your flipbooks and renders.

You can change to lower proxy sizes using presets.

1 Click the Globals tab in the Parameters workspace.

2   Expand the useProxy settings.

3   Cycle through the useProxy settings from Base to P1, P2, and P3.

By default, P1 is set to 0.5, 1 for its scale/aspect ratio; P2 is 0.25, 1; and P3 is 0.1, 1. The current proxy setting will appear in the associated text field.

Proxy Scale

Notice how the P1, P2, and P3 buttons automatically change the proxyScale parameters. Shake automatically computes proxy images based on a couple of Globals parameters. The primary parameter is the proxyScale variable. Not only will the proxy scale automatically downsize all of your input images, but it will also (behind the scenes) multiply all pixel-specific parameters such as pan or blur values by the same amount. The result is that you will end up with an image that is visually the same, other than the quality difference, at both low and high resolution.

When you activate a proxy, a proxy button illuminates at the top right of the title bar. You can use this button to quickly turn off proxies or return to any of the useProxy presets.

When generating proxy images on the fly, the following two things occur:

▶ All input images (such as FileIns) are zoomed down by the proxyScale amount. So if your proxy scale is ⅓, all images are zoomed by one-third. When you change the proxyScale in the interface, you will notice that image in the Viewer stays the same size onscreen. This is because Shake zooms the Viewer to compensate. The only perceptible difference is an apparent quality drop.

▶ These lower-resolution images are stored to a cache on your local disk, usually the temp folder, as they are created. Thus, they are available whenever they are needed. Currently, these images are generated only when required, so they're not created until you test a specific node. They also are generated only for the specific frame you are testing—when you move to a different frame, the proxies for that frame will be generated and cached. If you go back to the original frame, the proxies will already have been computed and will be immediately available.

1   Temporarily set the proxyScale back to the Base setting by clicking the Proxy button once on the top menu bar.

Now you can test your images at full resolution. This temporarily turns off the proxies.

2   Click the Proxy button once again to turn the proxies back on.

Keep in mind that using proxyScale is much different from simply appending a Zoom of the same value at the end of the script. The Zoom will calculate everything at full resolution and then perform the zoom-down at the end. Using proxies will prezoom all the input images (which may take some time) but will then perform all further operations at this reduced resolution, which is usually much faster.

TIP Always remember to reset useProxy to the Base setting before you render your final elements.

Proxy Ratio

Another proxy-related variable needs discussing—the proxyRatio parameter. It is needed only if you are working with images that are squeezed, such as anamorphic film images. This parameter, proxyRatio, allows proxies to be of a different aspect ratio from that of the original source images. It specifies the width-to-height ratio (relative to the original image) that you want for your proxies. Thus, if you have an anamorphic film frame that is squeezed by two times along the *x*-axis, you may want to set the proxyRatio to 0.5 to produce a proxy image that is unsqueezed or flattened.

NOTE ▶ By setting the proxyRatio, you actually change the resolution of your image; it is not a visualization change. If you don't want to change the resolution of your image, you can change the aspect ratio of the Viewer instead of the image with the Globals viewerAspectRatio parameter. This control is located in the Globals format group.

Customize P1, P2, and P3 Settings

You can customize the P1, P2, and P3 useProxy parameters for your script or session by opening the desired proxyDefaultFile in the Globals tab and modifying the proxyScale and proxyRatio parameters. For example, I prefer to work at ⅓ scale with film-resolution files.

1   Click the Globals tab and change the proxySet parameter from No_Precomputed_Proxies to Relative.

The Relative setting will save any generated proxies in a folder relative to your full-size file. This will make life easier when you get to the next section, "Generating Proxies."

2   Expand the proxy2DefaultFile group.

3   Set the proxy2DefaultScale to ⅓ and the proxy2DefaultBytes to 16 bits.

Because Shake treats Kodak Cineon 10-bit log files as 16-bit linear, it is best to keep the proxy in 16 bits as well.

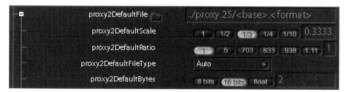

4   Change the proxy2DefaultFile name from *proxy.25* to *proxy.33*.

5   Remove one of the periods before the first slash (/) in the proxy2DefaultFile name.

Removing one of the periods ensures that proxies generated in the next exercise will be stored in a folder called proxy.33 in the Lesson08 folder.

The next step is to generate proxies based on your customized settings.

Generating Proxies

Up to this point, Shake has been automatically creating low-resolution equivalents of your high-resolution source images on the fly. But you might want to use another method when you are working on a project for a long time and will be doing many flipbook tests. In this case, why not pre-generate your proxies when you start the project with an initial rendering process? The proxy files will then be pulled from these precalculated images rather than being generated on the fly.

You can either pre-generate the files inside the interface, or load them up after they have been created by an external process. This is the workflow for generating proxies inside the Shake interface:

▶   Open the Globals useProxy subtree.

▶   Open the desired proxyDefaultFile subtree and set your scale, ratio, format, and bit depth parameters for the proxy (as you did in the previous steps).

▶   Set your paths for where the proxies should go with the proxyDefaultFile setting. For instance, if you are using the proxySet:Relative setting, the proxy1DefaultFile default file path is /proxy.50/<base>.<format>, which means they will go in a folder at the same level as the source images and will be given the same name with the same frame range and in the same format.

   <base> = image name + frame range

   <format> = format extension

▶   Read in your images with FileIn.

▶   Select the FileIns for which you want to generate proxies.

▶ Right-click one of the FileIn nodes and choose Render > Render Proxies. From this window, you can launch a render of your proxy files. Make sure to activate the button of the proxies you want to generate.

OK, let's generate some proxies. The proxy settings you entered in the previous steps are fine.

1   Highlight the glass node and right-click it.

2   Select Render > Render Proxies.

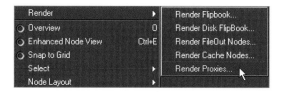

The Render Proxy Parameters window opens. Notice that all three Render proxyDefault parameters are turned off.

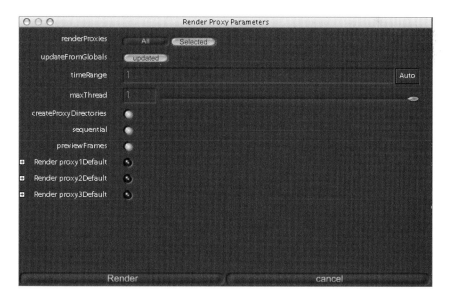

3   Click the Render proxy2Default button to activate it.

proxy2Default is the only set of proxies that you want to generate at this time.

4   Enter *1-19* in the timeRange parameter.

5   Click Render.

Proxies are rendered into a folder called proxy.33 inside the Lesson08 folder.

6   Activate the P2 useProxy setting.

A ⅓ resolution, 16-bit pre-generated proxy is shown on the screen. Yippee! But don't celebrate just yet. Proxies for your other elements have to be generated.

7   FileIn the **bullet.1-19.iff** and **reflection.1-19.iff** clips from the Lesson08 folder.

8   Select both the bullet and reflection nodes.

9   Repeat steps 2–5, and don't forget to set the timeRange parameter to *1-19*.

10 When the proxy render is finished, close both Monitor windows.

The Bullet Composite

Let's start by creating the composite using low-resolution proxies.

Getting Started

There is a Globals viewerZoom parameter that automatically keeps the image the same size in the Viewer regardless of what proxy setting you have selected. Sometimes this is a useful feature, but it often makes it difficult to set the image to a 1:1 zoom. For this lesson, it will be deactivated.

1   In the Globals tab, expand the format subtree.

2   Scroll down to the viewerZoom parameter and set it to a value of *1*.

3   Click the Home icon beneath the Viewer to view the clip at a 1:1 zoom ratio.

4   Switch the Viewer back to Normal Update mode.

5   Add a FileIn, and then browse to the Lesson08 folder and select P2 for the Load As Proxy parameter at the bottom of the FileIn window.

Because the **bullet_comp** clip doesn't have full-resolution images associated with it, and because it is the same size and format as the P2 proxy set, you can use the Load As Proxy parameter to specify that this clip is a proxy.

6   Double-click the **bullet_comp** clip in the FileIn window.

You should now have four clips in the Node workspace.

View the Clips

1   Set the timeRange in the Globals parameters automatically by clicking the Auto button.

2   Click the Home icon at the bottom right of the interface to set the Time Bar to the same time range.

3   Click the Fit Image to Viewer icon in the Viewer to reset the zoom of the Viewer.

4   Double-click the **bullet_comp** clip, click the Flipbook icon, and play it when it's done loading.

This is the final effect that you will be building. A computer-generated bullet has been composited into a scene of exploding glass.

5   Load the **bullet** and **reflection** clips into a flipbook and play them.

The **bullet** and **reflection** clips are both computer generated and have an alpha channel.

6   Load the **glass** clip into a flipbook and play it.

The live-action **glass** clip is the background for your composite. To reiterate, this clip is a Kodak 10-bit Cineon log clip. Clips that are in log space appear flattened, or compressed, in their highlights and shadows.

7   Close all the flipbooks when done.

Working with Kodak 10-Bit Cineon Files

OK, time to take a nap—here comes some digital film history. Way back when, Kodak came out with the Cineon file format to support its film scanners and recorders. Because computer processors were slow and disk space and RAM were expensive, Kodak developed an efficient color compression scheme based on the idea that the human eye is more sensitive to shadows and midtones than to highlights. The highlights could be compressed, saving the data in the file. That resulted in a smaller, 10-bit, file making those old computer systems run faster.

Shake generally assumes that you are working in linear color space simply because mathematical operators will yield different results when working in logarithmic color space. It does not, however, necessarily mean that logarithmic images are not handled. If you exclusively bring in log images, the result will also be a log image. However, operations that involve multiplying or dividing (Mult, Gamma, Over, and so on) may return unpredictable results because values are being unevenly pushed in the higher or lower ranges. The preferred method of operation is to always convert your log files into linear space with the LogLin command before adding further operations. You would then continue with your compositing tree until the end, when you would place a LogLin command at the bottom of your tree to convert the image back to logarithmic color space.

That is as complicated as this discussion will get. If you want to torture yourself further, you can refer to the Shake user manual for more information.

> **NOTE** ► If you choose to do color corrections or composites in log space, the results may be unpredictable.

1   Attach a LogLin function from the Color tab after the glass node.

LogLin performs either a log-to-linear or linear-to-log conversion. You can adjust the black and white points and gamma, as well as make color adjustments.

2   Set rOffset to a value of 6 and bOffset to −29.

This color adjustment makes the image a nice cool blue.

Adding the Bullet

Because the **bullet** clip has an alpha channel, you can composite it into the background scene with an Over function.

1   Go to frame 6.

2 Click the **bullet** clip to select it, and choose Over from the Layer tab.

3 Connect the output of LogLin1 to the second input of the Over1 node.

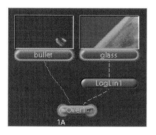

4 Drag the Time Bar to various frames to view your composite.

Popping Through the Glass

The **bullet** clip needs color correction and filtering to simulate it breaking through the hole in the glass.

1 Drag the Time Bar to frame 3.

Go back in time and recall the premultiplication discussion in Lesson 2, "Basic Compositing." Prior to color-correcting a premultiplied element, which includes almost all computer-generated elements, you must divide it by its matte with an MDiv (Matte Divide) node.

2 Add an MDiv node from the Color tab between the bullet and Over1.

3 Select a Fade node from the Color tab.

Fade is similar to Brightness, but it also affects the alpha channel.

4 Double-click the Over1 node and activate preMultiply.

5 Click the right side of Fade1 to edit its parameters.

6 Set the value to *0.45*.

The entire bullet darkens and fades, as it should, but we want to affect only the lower half. Sounds like RotoShape is coming to the rescue.

7 Click Create to the right of the Mask parameter.

A RotoShape node is created and automatically connected to the Mask input of the Fade1 node.

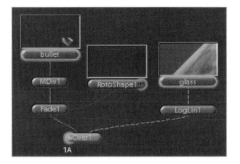

8 Set the Res parameters to *1828x988* and draw a shape like the one in the following image.

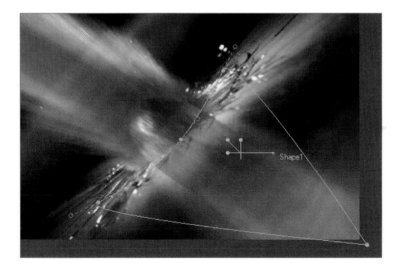

9 Double-click the Over1 node.

It's looking good, but the edge of the shape is too hard.

10 From the Filter tab, add a Blur node after RotoShape1 and set the pixels to a value of *50*.

11 Go to frame 1.

The only thing that bugs me is that the bullet is too sharp before it pops through the glass.

12 Insert a Blur after Fade1 and set the pixels to *10*.

The RotoShape used to mask the Fade node can also be used to mask the blur, so that it affects only the bullet when it is behind the glass.

13 Connect the output of Blur1 to the Mask input of Blur2.

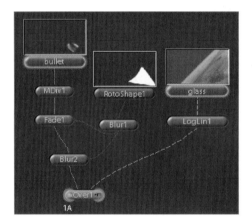

14 Create a flipbook of the Over1 node.

The bullet now appears to be busting through the glass.

Color-Correcting the Bullet

The bullet image looks flat to me. Adding some contrast would really help it.

1 Go to frame 6.

2 Highlight Blur2 and insert a ContrastLum node from the Color tab.

3 Set the value to *1.8* and the center to *0.2*.

Setting the center to a lower value like 0.2 produces a brighter image. This correction matches the overall shadows and highlights of the glass image, but I really don't care for the bright edges around the bullet.

You can fix this problem by isolating and correcting only the edge of the bullet.

4   Select the bullet node and from the Filter tab, Shift-click EdgeDetect to create a new branch.

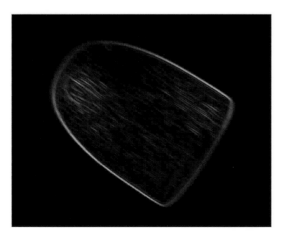

EdgeDetect is great for extracting and massaging edges. You can control what is detected, how strong the edge is, and how much it can expand or soften. Unfortunately, you can't choose what channel of the original image the edge is created from. In this case, the edge is created from the RGB channels and shows texturing in the center of the bullet. We only want the edges, which we can get from the bullet's alpha channel.

5   Right-click a Reorder node on the Color tab and select Create.

6   Drag the Reorder1 node directly over the connecting line between the bullet and EdgeDetect1 so that both its knots appear highlighted.

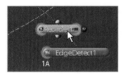

7   When you release the mouse button, the node is inserted automatically.

8   Type *aaa* in the Channels parameter.

9   View the EdgeDetect1 node.

We now have a usable edge matte.

10 From the Color tab, insert a Brightness node after ContrastLum1 and connect EdgeDetect1 to the Mask input.

11 View Over1 while editing Brightness1.

12 Set the value to *0.25* and watch only the edge darken.

Oh baby, it's starting to steam.

The Final Touches

I bet you are thinking, Hey, I'm almost done! But no, the slimy producer guy wants the bullet to be enveloped within the spray of glass. Well, admit it, it's a good idea.

All right, all right. If you make a luminance matte of the spraying glass high-lights and composite those portions of the glass over what you have done so far, the bullet will be surrounded by shards of glass.

1 Drag the Time Bar to frame 5.

2 Select LogLin1 and from the Key tab, Shift-click LumaKey to create a new branch.

LumaKey creates a key in the alpha channel based on overall luminance. Values below loVal are set to black, and values above hiVal are set to white.

3 Activate matteMult and set loVal to *0.35*.

4   From the Layer tab, add an Over node after LumaKey1 and connect Over1 to the right input of Over2.

Much better. The glass spray is partially around the bullet. Just add a reflection and some film grain to wrap it up.

5   From the Layer tab, select a Screen node and hook the reflection to the right input.

The Screen node is particularly handy for reflections and luminescent elements, like the reflection element, as it preserves the highlights. The bullet reflection is subtle but effective. Finally, add film grain to the bullet. You gotta have the film grain.

6   Highlight Brightness1 and from the Filter tab, select a Film Grain node.

7   Set both the intensity and grainSize to *0.5*.

Here's your tree so far:

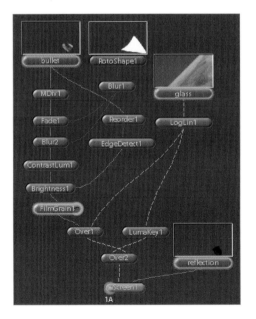

8   Double-click Screen1 and make a flipbook.

It looks real to me.

Convert Back to Log Space

The last part of this process is to convert the Screen1 output back to log color space. Remember when you added a LogLin node to convert the bullet shot from log to linear color space? Now you have to undo it and convert the entire composite back to log space.

1   Add a LogLin node from the Color tab after Screen1.

2   Change the conversion parameter to Lin to Log.

Rendering Full Resolution

You now have a script based on using low-resolution proxies. Before the final render takes place, switch the Globals parameter useProxy to the Base setting.

1   Set the Globals parameter useProxy back to the Base setting by clicking the Proxy button on the top menu bar.

2   Place your cursor over the Viewer and press the F key to fit the image to the Viewer.

The script looks exactly as it did before, except now the FileIns have loaded the high-resolution versions. That's the beauty of this system. You can quickly work out your composite using lower-resolution proxies and then, with the click of a button, switch back to your high-resolution originals. If this were a real job, you'd be ready to render. It's not a real job, so you're done.

3   Quit Shake.

Lesson Review

1.   What are proxies?

2.   Describe the Kodak Cineon 10-bit logarithmic file format.

3.   Which node converts logarithmic images to linear images?

4.   To what color space should you convert logarithmic files?

Answers

1.   Proxies are lower-resolution images that you substitute for your high-resolution images so you can work faster.

2.   The Kodak Cineon 10-bit logarithmic file format uses an efficient color compression scheme based on the idea that the human eye is more sensitive to shadows and midtones than to highlights.

3. The LogLin function converts logarithmic images to linear images and vice versa.

4. You should always convert your logarithmic files into linear space.

9

Lesson 9
Video/Audio

This lesson introduces you to the way Shake handles audio files and video images. In particular, you'll learn about video fields, interlacing, 3:2 pull-down, and field rendering.

Here are two consecutive video frames split into four fields. Interlacing weaves fields together.

Video Fields

A review of the mechanics of video frames and fields is in order, so listen up. The resolution of video images is 525 lines for NTSC and 625 lines for PAL. NTSC video runs at 30 frames per second, and PAL at 25 fps. Each video frame is made of two separate subframes called *fields*. Each of these fields is an individual snapshot in time. By using fields, the viewer sees twice as many frames and perceives smoother motion. Even though the fields represent different points in time, they occupy the same video frame. This is achieved through a process called *interlacing*—a thorn in the side of graphic artists and compositors everywhere.

The following pictures show two consecutive video frames with interlaced fields of a skier flying through the air. The more motion an image has, the more interlacing you will see.

Frame 1

Frame 2

Here are the same two images split into four fields:

Frame 1 Field 1

Frame 1 Field 2

Frame 2 Field 1

Frame 2 Field 2

Here comes the fun part. Interlacing weaves together the two fields by starting at the top of the image and using one line from field 1 (the odd-numbered field) and another line from field 2 (the even field) until all 525 or 625 lines are interlaced together. Temporally, the fields always occur in the order of field 1 and then field 2. Spatially, the ordering is different for NTSC and PAL. For NTSC, the spatial field order starts with field 2, or the even field. For PAL, it is the opposite—field 1, the odd field, is the first spatial field.

Therefore, the interlace process produces two fields of half-height for every broadcast frame. When a television displays these images, it quickly shows the first field only, and then the second field only, and then it proceeds to the next frame. This solution is interesting because each field sacrifices vertical resolution for the benefit of temporal quality.

Importing Interlaced Images

When importing interlaced images, you need to be aware of the FileIn node's deInterlacing parameter. When enabled, it separates the two fields from each other, placing field 1 at frame 1, and field 2 at frame 1.5. Each field is then copied and moved into the empty spatial place of the removed field. This ensures that all spatial effects are handled properly when fields are rendered. This strategy is clever because it doubles the number of frames you have but keeps the frames within the same duration. Go figure.

1 Open Shake.

2 FileIn the **ski1.1-15.iff** sequence from the Lesson09 folder.

3 Set the Globals timeRange to *1-15*.

4 While you're at it, click the Home icon at the bottom right of the screen to make the Time Bar's low and high values match the Globals timeRange.

5 Step through the clip with the left and right arrow keys.

Notice how the skier is interlaced as he flies.

6 In the FileIn parameter controls, click the deInterlacing parameter until it says Even.

Even is for NTSC, and Odd is for PAL.

7   In the Time Bar, change the Inc (increment) parameter from 1 to *0.5*.

8   Step through the clip again with the left and right arrow keys.

The skier now moves on each field in half-frame increments.

NOTE ▶ If you step through the clip and the image seems to stutter every other field, switch your deInterlacing to Odd if you are on Even and to Even if you are on Odd. The motion should then be continuous. Field order varies depending on the television standard.

It isn't always necessary to deinterlace video. However, it is helpful to deinterlace when you need to paint on individual fields, animate parameters, transform images, track motion, and create traveling mattes with the RotoShape node.

Common Problems with Interlaced Images

Interlacing creates two particular types of problems for digital image manipulation.

The first problem occurs when you have any animated parameter. The animation must be understood and applied at half-frame intervals. If you read in an interlaced clip and apply a static color correction, no problems occur because both fields receive the same correction. If, however, you animate the color correction, you must turn on the Globals parameter fieldRendering in order to evaluate the correct set of lines at the appropriate interpolated value.

The second and trickier problem happens with any node that has spatial effects, like a Blur or a Move2D. If you pan an image up by one pixel in Y, you have effectively reversed time, because the even lines are moved to the odd field, and the odd lines are moved to the even field. The clip will have extremely jerky movement, since every two fields are reversed.

Field Rendering

To correct the problems I've described, you can use fieldRendering in the renderControls of the Globals tab. With fieldRendering turned on, Shake separates the rendering into two separate fields. All animation and spatial effects are allocated to the proper fields. Why don't you give it a try?

1 Attach a Move2D node from the Transform tab to the ski1 clip.

2 Go to frame 1 of the clip.

3 Open the Scale subtree and turn on the Keyframe toggle for the xScale parameter.

The yScale parameter is automatically linked to the xScale parameter because of Shake's default parameter linking. Therefore, it doesn't need to be animated.

4 Set the xScale parameter to a value of *0*.

5 Go to frame 8 and set the xScale parameter to a value of *1*.

6 Step through frames 8 to 1.

As you step through the frames, the Move2D animation that you created animates in half-frame increments. This is good.

7   Click the Flipbook icon and view your animation.

The flipbook shows something quite different. There is motion only on the individual frames. This is bad. If you want to render on individual fields, you must turn on fieldRendering.

8   Go to the Globals tab and scroll down to the renderControls. Expand them by clicking the +.

There are three fieldRendering settings:

▶   0—Off.

▶   1—Field rendering with the odd field first. This is generally the setting for PAL images.

▶   2—Field rendering with the even field first. This is generally the setting for NTSC images.

9   Toggle fieldRendering until it says Even.

10   Step through frames 1 to 8 again.

The Move2D animation is now field-interlaced, and it will result in a nice, smooth animation when it is placed back onto videotape.

You don't have to use field rendering when you import interlaced images and apply static color corrections. For all other functions, or if you animate any value, you should turn on fieldRendering. The fieldRendering handles all transformations, filters, and warps by internally removing the intermediate black lines from each field, and then resizing the Y resolution back up to full frame. Shake does this for each field and then interlaces them back together again.

3:2 Pull-Down

The other type of video interlacing issue that you will need to contend with is 3:2 pull-down. What exactly does *pull-down* mean? It is a technique to temporally convert film footage to video footage and back again. This pull-down is introduced during the film-to-video transfer process. Given that film uses solid frames and video uses interlaced fields, and that film runs at 24 fps and NTSC runs at 30 fps, you split the film footage into fields and double up two out of five frames to increase your frames to fill the 30 fps.

The Pulldown parameters in the Timing section of the FileIn node allow you to manage the pull-down of a sequence.

The phrase *30 to 24* means that you have received a film sequence that has been transferred at 30 fps. You now want to return it to 24 fps. *24 to 30* means that you want to convert 24 fps film footage to 30 fps. Both allow you to select which field will dominate. Typically, PAL is odd and NTSC is even.

Here's the classic diagram illustrating this phenomenon:

Four film frames

Convert to:

Five video frames

The third and fourth video frames have blended fields to stretch out time. It's called 3:2 because you have three solid frames and two mixed frames.

You can fully reconstruct your original four film frames by extracting the field data from the five video frames. Therein lies the rub. When you receive your footage, it has probably been edited and all of the clips have been shifted around, so frames 3 and 4 aren't necessarily the mixed frames. You therefore need to figure out which is the first frame before you attempt to remove the extra fields.

To do this, go to the first five frames in your sequence. If the first frame with field blending in it is frame 3, you know your firstFrame should be set to AA in the Timing section of your FileIn node. If the first frame with field blending is frame 2, you know your first frame is BB and can set your firstFrame parameter accordingly. If your first frames have no motion or are a solid color and you just can't figure it out, you have to jump to a time range of frames that display the blending and start guessing at firstFrame until the fields go away. Very scientific, isn't it?

> **NOTE ▶** Removing 3:2 pull-down from clips transferred from film to video is not a requirement. However, it is very helpful to remove pull-down when tracking, integrating multiple clips, or creating traveling mattes with the RotoShape node. The preferred workflow is to remove 3:2 pull-down from all of your source material, composite the effect, and then add 3:2 pull-down to the final shot when done.

1   Go to frame 1 and set the Time Bar back to incrementing by *1* frame.

2   Set the fieldRendering toggle of the Globals tab's renderControls parameter to the Off position.

3   FileIn the **ski2.1-37.iff** clip from the Lesson09 folder.

4   Set the Globals timeRange to *1-37.*

5   Step through the first five frames of the sequence.

The first frame is interlaced, but three solid frames follow before the next interlaced frame.

6   Look at the diagram of the five video frames earlier in this section, and you'll see that the first frame of this sequence would be considered a CD frame.

NOTE ▶ If a clip doesn't contain motion, you won't see any interlacing.

7 Click the Timing tab in the Parameters workspace and scroll down.

8 In the Pulldown parameter, click the 30 to 24 button.

This will convert your 30 fps clip into a 24 fps clip using the AA frame as the first frame in the sequence.

9 Change the firstFrame parameter to CD to match the pull-down cadence of the **ski2** clip.

10 Click Auto in the Globals tab to reset the timeRange to reflect the new timing of the compressed **ski2** clip.

timeRange   1-29   Auto

11 Create a flipbook and click Play.

Pull-down frames are removed, changing the original 37-frame clip to 29 frames.

12 Close the flipbook.

Remastering Media in the FileIn Node

The FileIn Convert parameter provides a method for converting footage from one format to another using advanced image-processing algorithms to deinterlace, rescale, and retime the incoming shot. In this lesson, you'll start with an HD (high definition) image sequence and convert it to a standard-definition NTSC clip. You can also convert from and to film, NTSC, PAL, and HD image sequences.

You have access to a series of parameters in the FileIn node that allow you to change the frame rate, resize the output resolution, anti-alias and sharpen the resulting image, and deinterlace the media being referenced by that FileIn.

These conversion options provide the highest-quality method of resizing and deinterlacing available in Shake, far superior to the normal transform nodes that are available from the tool tabs. These options are available only within the FileIn node.

1   Select File > New Script and answer No when asked whether to save.

File	Edit	Tools	Viewers	R
New script			⌘N	
Open script...			⌘O	

2   FileIn the **plane.1-37.iff** sequence from the Lesson09 folder.

3   Place your pointer over the Viewer and press the F key to fit the image.

The plane clip is a 1920x1080 60i HD clip—*60i* means it is 30 frames per second, with each frame containing 2 fields.

4   Set the Globals timeRange to *1-37*.

5   Step through a few frames of the clip.

It's pretty obvious that the clip has interlaced video fields.

Using the FileIn > Timing > reTiming > Convert parameter, you can easily change this interlaced HD resolution clip to a deinterlaced NTSC clip.

6   Click the Timing tab in the FileIn parameters.

7   Scroll down and click the reTiming parameter's Convert button.

There are a number of parameters to choose from, but essentially all you need to do is set your input and output frame rates as well as the output resolution.

8   In the InputFrameRate text field, type *30* for the frames per second and press Enter.

The OuputFrameRate can be left at the default setting, which matches the InputFrameRate.

9   Expand the InputFrameRate subtree.

10   Click the InputFrameInterlaced toggle to blend the interlaced frames.

Shake will take a moment before the Viewer is updated.

11   Type *720* and *486* as the OutputRes parameters, pressing Enter after each entry.

The Viewer displays what the final clip will look like.

The Motion and Deinterlacing parameters offer you the choice between Best and Fast. The Best setting takes significantly longer to process, and the increase in quality is often undetectable at higher resolutions. Always try the Fast setting first.

12 Create a flipbook and play the clip once it is done processing.

This will take a moment, so feel free to make some prank phone calls while it is processing. The result is a high-quality resize operation with all interlacing artifacts removed. This is a very versatile function, which makes the conversion of clips from one medium to another a breeze.

13 Close the flipbook.

Some other useful Convert parameters to note are:

▶ AntiAlias—When you're scaling media up, turn this parameter on to improve the quality of conversions.

▶ Details—This built-in sharpening control lets you add detail back to an enlarged image.

Miscellaneous Video Functions

Shake has several other video-oriented functions. Keep in mind that these operate with the assumption that fieldRendering is off, since they would be affected by the field rendering options in the same manner as other functions are. These functions include the following:

Tab	Function	Action
Globals	timecodeMode	Sets the timecode format displayed in the Time Bar.
Time Bar	T on keyboard	Toggles timecode/frame display.
Image	FileIn	Has deinterlacing, as well as pull-down/pull-up capabilities under the Timing subtree.
Color	VideoSafe	Limits your colors to video-legal ranges.
Layer	Interlace	Interlaces two images, pulling one field from one image and the second field from the other image; you can select field dominance.
Other	Deinterlace	Retains one field from an image and creates the other field from it; you have three choices for how this is done. The height of the image remains the same.
Other	Field	Strips out one field, turning the image into a half-height image.
Other	Swapfields	Switches the even and odd fields of an image when fieldRendering is off.

Audio

Audio normally plays second fiddle in most visual effects software and is affectionately referred to as "the junk you drag along with the picture." Fortunately, Shake has some nice tools to handle this junk.

Shake can read AIFF and WAV files, mix them together, extract curves based on an audio waveform, manipulate the timing of the sound, and save the files again. These audio curves can be visualized in the Curve Editor.

> **NOTE** ▶ Shake supports PCM AIFF and PCM WAV files. Although multiple frequencies and bit-depth importation is supported, playback is always 44.1 kHz, 16 bits at Medium quality, and export is always at Highest quality.

Loading and Playing Audio Files

1   Select File > New Script and answer No when prompted whether to save the script.

2   Click the Audio Panel tab in the Node View.

The Audio Panel appears on the Node View.

3   Click the Open Audio File button at the top left of the Audio Panel.

4   When the File Browser opens, select **citroen_c4.aiff** from the Lesson09 folder.

The **citroen_c4.aiff** audio file loads into the Audio Panel and is ready to play.

5   Click the Preview Audio button.

The Preview Audio button plays the audio file, and you should see the audio level displayed on the meters.

NOTE ▶ Because audio playback is handled through the use of Macintosh-specific QuickTime libraries, you can hear audio playback only on a Macintosh OS X system. However, you can still analyze and visualize audio on a Linux system. I have always preferred to see sound rather than hear it.

Enabling, Viewing, and Editing Audio

Now that you have some sound, it would be nice to play it with an image.

1   FileIn the **robot_comp.1-60.iff** sequence from the Lesson09 folder.

The **robot_comp** is the same shot you worked on in Lessons 2 and 3.

2   In the Globals tab, set the timeRange to *1-60*.

3   Click the Home icon at the bottom right of the Time Bar to set the sequence to the Globals timeRange.

4   To activate the audio, click the Audio Playback button on the Time Bar ...

... and click the Play button to the right of it.

The audio and video play at the same time in the Viewer. The playback speed will depend on the speed of your hard drive and the size of the image.

5   Stop the audio playback with the Stop button to the right of the Time Bar.

TIP   You can scrub the audio at any time by Control-dragging on the Time Bar.

Now that you can hear the audio, would you like to see it? The audio waveform can be displayed in the Curve Editor and slipped in time, which means that you can change its position relative to frame1 of the Time Bar.

6   Select the Curve Editor in the tool tabs and activate the Curve Editor's Draw Waveform toggle.

The following image is an example of an audio waveform viewed in the Curve Editor.

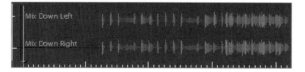

7   To slip all audio tracks in time, Shift-Option-drag inside the Curve Editor.

The audio channels are slipped in time.

NOTE ▶ You can also change the timing of an audio file by first making sure that it is selected in the Audio Panel and then adjusting the Time Shift parameter.

8   In the Audio Panel, set the Time Shift parameter to a value of *–509*.

This syncs the audio to the video. I just happened to know that 509 frames would do the trick. I know everything.

9   Click the Play button at the bottom right of the Time Bar.

10 Click the Stop button when done.

Mixing and Exporting Sound

You can control how sound files are mixed together in the Mixdown Options subtree in the Audio Panel. Once finished, you can export the result to disk. Before you can mix audio, you will need to load a couple more audio files.

1   Click the Open Audio File button at the top left of the Audio Panel.

2   When the File Browser opens, select **air_release.aiff** from the Lesson09 folder.

3   Click the Open Audio File button again and select **motor_lift.aiff**.

Three audio files are now loaded in the Audio Panel.

4   Click the Preview Audio button to hear the three tracks at once.

The motor_lift sounds a little too loud, and it could also start a little later.

5   Enter a value of –8 in the Track Gain parameter.

Because the **motor_lift.aiff** file is already selected, the Track Gain parameter will adjust only that sound.

6   Set the Time Shift parameter to *20* so that the motor_lift sound starts later.

7   Click the Preview Audio button again to hear your new mix.

Much better, because the motor_lift sound no longer drowns out the music. If you wanted to save the mixdown to a new file, just open the Mixdown Options subtree and set the appropriate options—the most important of which are the filename and location for the new file and the Time Range. Once you click the Save Mixdown button, Shake renders out the new audio file. Sounds good!

Extracting Curves from Audio Files

The Create Curves subtree lets you analyze the current audio mix, creating a keyframed curve that is stored as the Audio parameter located within the Globals > localParameters subtree.

This curve can then be used by other functions in Shake as a standard expression allowing the synchronization of nearly any animated parameter to the audio waveform. The use of expressions and parameter linking will be discussed in detail in Lesson 12.

Go ahead, create an audio curve.

1   Open the Create Curves subtree.

2   Click the Update from Globals button to set the Timerange to match the timeRange parameter of your project.

3   Click the Create Variable Under Globals button to create the audio parameter.

A progress bar appears.

4 Open the Globals > localParameters subtree to reveal the Audio parameter that has been created.

This parameter is now ready for use as an expression within a Shake node.

5 Switch back to the Node View tab.

6 Select the **robot_comp** clip and add a CameraShake node from the Transform tab.

CameraShake applies random noise to pan values simulating camera shaking.

7 In the Frequency parameter, type *audio* and press Enter.

8 Click the Play button at the bottom right of the Time Bar.

The camera shaking is now synchronized to the waveform of the audio. How cool is that?

9 Press the Stop button when done.

10 Quit Shake.

Lesson Review

1. What makes up a video frame?

2. Can you describe the spatial ordering of fields in NTSC and PAL?

3. Define *pull-down*.

4. List some of the audio file formats you can use in Shake and what you can do with them.

5. How do you change the timing of an audio file?

Answers

1. Each frame of video is made up of two separate subframes called fields.

2. For NTSC, the spatial field order starts with field 2, the even-number field. For PAL, it is the opposite: field 1, the odd field, is the first spatial field.

3. Pull-down is a technique to temporally convert film footage to video footage and back again.

4. Shake can read AIFF and WAV files, mix them together, extract curves based on an audio waveform, manipulate the timing of the sound, and save out the files again.

5. You can change the timing of an audio file by first making sure that it is selected in the Audio Panel and then adjusting the Time Shift parameter.

10

Lesson Files	APTS_Shake > essons > Lesson10
Media	bg.1-58.iff
	gs.1-58.iff
	gs_comp.1-58.iff
	reflection.1-58.iff
Time	This lesson takes approximately 1 hour to complete.
Goals	Demonstrate the basic theory of the Primatte chroma-keying system
	Use Primatte to generate keys
	Process large image files faster with a DOD (Domain of Definition)

Lesson 10
Keying

Keying and generating mattes is one of the most important aspects of compositing. The process of *keying* involves extracting an object from an image and combining it with a different background. Most keyers use the difference in color between the color channels of an image to extract the matte. Normally, this technique depends on the foreground subject being photographed in front of a uniformly colored background, such as a blue or green screen. Shake includes the Primatte and Keylight keyers, with the Ultimatte keyer available as an optional plug-in.

In this lesson you will use Primatte to key this image.

Understanding Primatte

In this lesson, we'll use Photron's Primatte chroma-keying system. To use Primatte effectively, you need to understand the application and how it works. Primatte constructs a 3D space defined by three concentric partial spheres. Through a series of color scrubs, Primatte places colors along red, green, or blue axes in the 3D space and assigns them to one of four different zones.

Zone 1 is the complete background image; zone 2 is the foreground image with spill suppression and transparency; zone 3 is the foreground image with spill suppression; and zone 4 is the complete foreground image, 100 percent opaque with no spill suppression. As you scrub on an image, Primatte pushes and pulls on the partial spheres based on which function you use, creating dents and bumps on the surfaces. The position of the dents is determined by the pixel values as located on the RGB axes.

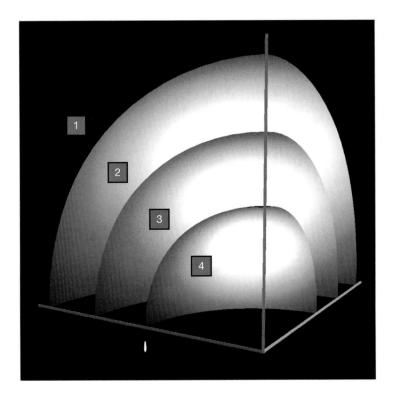

Visualizing a Primatte key in 3D color space would look something like this:

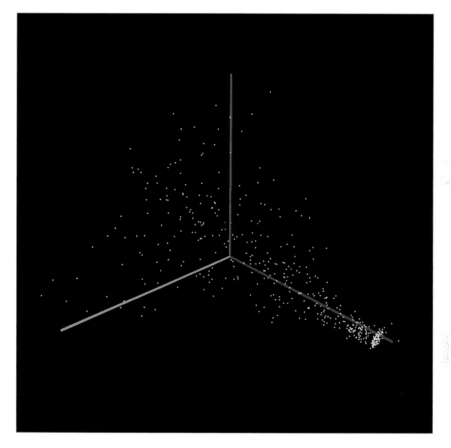

Pixels are distributed according to their color values and are manipulated based on their positioning within that 3D space.

Primatte Functions

Each Primatte function assigns pixels to a certain zone:

▶   Background—When this mode is selected, the sampled pixels within the image window are pixels known to be 100 percent background. The matte is completely black.

- ▶ Foreground—When this mode is selected, the sampled pixels within the image window become 100 percent foreground. The color of the sampled pixels are the same color as in the original foreground image. The matte is completely white.

- ▶ Fine Tuning: spillSponge—When this mode is selected, the cursor motion in the spillSponge slider performs a color adjustment of the sampled color against the background. After sampling a color region from the image, the farther to the right the cursor moves, the less of the foreground color component (or spill) is included in that color region. The farther to the left the cursor moves, the closer the color component of the selected region will be to the original foreground image. This is similar to the more automatic but less controllable individual Spill Sponge operator.

- ▶ Fine Tuning: fgTrans—This mode adjusts the transparency of the matte against the sampled color. After sampling a color region from the image, the farther to the right the cursor is, the more transparent the matte becomes in that color region. This is equivalent to Make FG Trans but offers more control.

- ▶ Fine Tuning: detailTrans—This determines the transparency of the sampled color, which is closer to the background color. The slider in this mode is useful for restoring the color of pixels that are faded because of a similarity to the background color. If you slide to the left, picked areas are more opaque. This is equivalent to Restore Detail but offers more control.

- ▶ Matte Sponge—This is used to restore foreground areas lost during spill suppression. It affects only the alpha channel.

The following are more automatic but less controllable functions:

- ▶ Spill Sponge—This affects the color of the foreground but not the matte. It suppresses the color you pick. This is usually used on spill areas that are known to be opaque, such as blue spill on the face or body. If the change is too drastic, supplement or replace the operation with Fine Tuning: spillSponge.

▶ Make FG Trans—This gives foreground material more transparency and is used for adjusting elements such as clouds or smoke. It is the equivalent of Fine Tuning: fgTrans, except it has no slider control.

▶ Restore Detail—This removes transparency on background material. It is useful for restoring lost details such as hair. It is the equivalent of Fine Tuning: detailTrans but doesn't have a slider.

If you are interested in delving further into Primatte, visit www.primatte.com. The site has an excellent white paper with enough technical information to make your head spin.

Viewing Your Clips

Before you begin, you'll need to load the clips.

1   Open Shake.

2   Click FileIn on the Image tab and select the **bg.1-58.iff**, **gs.1-58.iff**, **gs_comp.1-58.iff**, and **reflection.1-58.iff** clips from the Lesson10 folder.

All of these clips are 1920x1080 (HD resolution), so they take longer to load and will take a bit longer to process. It's probably a good idea to use a proxy.

3   Click the Proxy button and select P2.

This sets the proxy resolution to ¼, which will speed up processing. You can now view the final shot.

4 Place your cursor over the Viewer and press the F key.

This fits the image to the Viewer.

5 Go to the Globals tab and set the timeRange to *1-58*.

6 Click the Home icon on the bottom right of the interface to set the Time Bar to the same range as the Globals.

7 Double-click the **gs_comp** clip to select it.

8 Click the Flipbook icon and play the clip.

For this shot, you will create a key of the woman and place her over a background. Then, you will add a moving reflection element after stabilizing its motion.

9   Close this flipbook and make another one of the **gs** clip.

This is your green screen element, and boy, it's a doozy. The unevenly lit background and the amount of grain will present a real challenge.

10   Double-click the **bg** clip to see it in the Viewer.

The background is your standard industrial metal background—hand-forged, no doubt, by Old World artisans.

Creating the Key

When you create a key, also known as a matte, the foreground object that you are attempting to extract should be white in the alpha channel. The colored areas of the blue or green screen ideally would appear as black in the alpha channel. Elements such as smoke would likely have some transparency and show up as gray.

1   Drag the Time Bar to frame 55.

2   From the Key tab, right-click the Primatte node and choose Create.

You probably noticed that the Primatte node has quite a few inputs.

Primatte Inputs, from Left to Right

Parameter	Function
Foreground	This is the blue or green screen image.
Background	This is the background image.
garbageMatte	This is used to get rid of rigging or other elements you want to be transparent when they are otherwise not pulled by the keying operation.
holdoutMatte	This is a matte input for areas that you want to be opaque.
defocusedFg	This is used to create a blurred version of the blue screen to help deal with grain variation for film plates; typically you would attach a Blur node to the blue screen footage and insert it here.
replaceImage	You can do spill suppression with a solid color, with the background image (when no replaceImage is supplied), or with an alternate replaceImage to supply the color that will go into spill-suppressed areas. Common inputs for this are bg, bg with Blur applied to it, fg with Blur applied to it, fg with Monochrome applied to it, or fg with AdjustHSV attached to it.

3   Connect the **gs** clip to the far-left input of the Primatte node and the **bg** clip to the second input.

The Primatte node has a lot of parameters, so it's a good idea to change the layout of your interface.

4   Click the dividing line between the Parameters workspace and the Node workspace, and drag the line up to give yourself more room in the Parameters workspace.

The interface should look like this:

Now you can see all the parameters without having to scroll the window.
Primatte works by picking a Center value, meaning the average color of
the key you want to pull. Primatte is ready to scrub your background color
as soon as you add the node.

5   In the Viewer, drag across a small section of the green screen.

Initially nothing will happen, because Primatte is set to output Alpha Only
by default. If you are not viewing the alpha channel in the Viewer, you
won't see anything. If you want to see the composite, switch from Alpha
Only to Comp in the Output parameters.

6   In the Output parameters, click Comp.

You can now see a preliminary composite. It needs work—lots
of work.

The matte is weak, so the woman looks like a ghost.

7   Set the Output mode back to Alpha Only.

8   Look at the alpha channel in the Viewer.

You will notice that there are gray values for both the woman image and
the background.

9   Click the Foreground button and drag across the gray areas of the
woman's face.

foreground

This step tells Primatte to consider the gray pixels in the woman's face as foreground (opaque) material. As you have probably figured, it's going to take more than one swipe to remove the gray values inside the face, but don't go crazy. Each swipe produces a "harder," more opaque matte. Making the key too hard, either in the black background or white foreground areas, will result in lousy edges. Your goal is to remove as much of the gray as possible. The rest we will take care of with rotoshapes.

10 Repeat the previous step multiple times until most of the gray areas within the woman's face are gone by clicking the Foreground operator and then sampling areas in the Viewer.

After your foreground swipes, your alpha channel should look something like the image on the following page.

Because background gray values also exist, you should click the Background button and drag that away as well. Do this even if you can't see any impurity in the background. Your monitor will often disguise noise hiding in the background. This is not a problem here, however.

11 Click the Background button and drag to the right of the woman's left shoulder (screen right), being careful not to scrub into the completely white areas.

12 Click the Background button again and drag to the right of the woman's left ear (screen right).

> **NOTE** ▶ For foreground and background scrubs, you can drag as much as you want. For the other scrubs, use very fine, short scrubs.

After your background swipes, your matte should look like this:

Tuning Your Matte

Using rotoshapes, we will create a garbage matte for the areas of the background that should be transparent (black in the alpha channel) and a holdout matte for inside areas of the face that should be opaque (completely white in the alpha channel). These shapes can be plugged directly in to the Primatte inputs.

Garbage mattes are used to mask off unwanted areas of the background like set equipment or crewmembers eating doughnuts; holdout mattes are used to fill in holes within the interior of the matte.

1 Select a RotoShape node from the Image tab.

2 Set the Res parameter to *1920x1080*.

3 Click the left side of the Primatte node so that you can see the alpha channel.

4   Draw a shape that surrounds the gray and white values in the background.

This shape will be used for the garbage matte.

5   Select Main mode from the RotoShape Viewer toolbar and pull out a point over the woman's right shoulder (screen left).

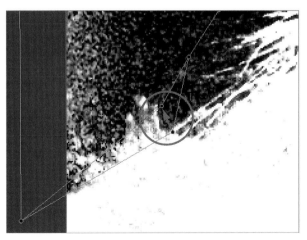

A soft edge is created in this region of the rotoshape.

6   Watch the magic happen as you connect the output of RotoShape1 to Primatte's garbageMatte input—the third input from the left.

The garbage matte removes the unwanted areas from the background. The holdout matte is next and will fill in the foreground areas of the woman.

7   Select another RotoShape node from the Image tab.

8   Set the Res parameter to *1920x1080*.

9   View the Primatte node while editing RotoShape2.

10 Draw a shape around the inside of the woman similar to the shape below.

She moves slightly from right to left, so don't draw too close to her edge.

11 Connect the output of RotoShape2 to Primatte's holdOutMatte input—the fourth input from the left.

The foreground is filled in with the area of the shape. Our matte is actually starting to look like it's going to work.

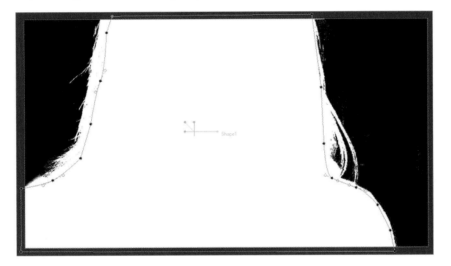

12 Click the Proxy button to deactivate it.

When performing keying functions, it is best to double-check your results every once in a while at full resolution, as the proxy can hide imperfections in the matte.

13 Set the Output parameter to Comp.

14 Look at the RGB channels in the Viewer.

When working at full resolution, you can activate the Viewer DOD (Domain of Definition).

The Viewer DOD isolates an area and speeds up all image processes.

15 Turn on the Viewer DOD button in the Viewer toolbar.

16 Drag the corner handles to crop the image.

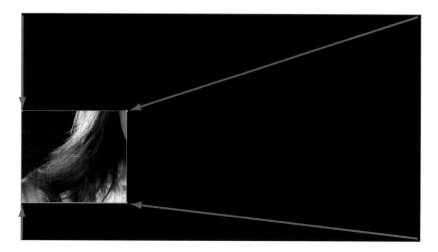

Now, take away some green spill from the woman's hair.

17 Zoom in to the woman's hair.

18 Click the right side of the Primatte node to reload its parameters.

19 Select Spill Sponge and scrub a green strand of the woman's hair.

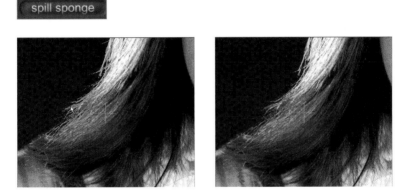

The green spill is removed.

20 Click the Active button to toggle the spill sponge operation on and off to see what it is doing. Leave the Active button on when you are done.

You may want to use Fine Tuning: spillSponge instead, because it gives you more control.

21 Click Delete Op to remove the spill sponge operation.

Undo and Primatte are not on speaking terms, but if you are using the trial version of Shake, you don't know what Undo is anyway. You are in luck nonetheless: To remove an operator, just click the Delete Op button.

22 Drag the currentOp slider all the way to the left.

Notice how you toggle through the operations you have already performed.
By parking the currentOp slider at a particular point, you can modify,
delete, or insert a new operation. Nice, huh?

23 Click evalToEnd to turn it off, and drag the currentOp slider back and forth.

Turning off evalToEnd shows you the Primatte composite only up to the
operation that you are parked on. This helps you examine all the various
steps that went into the creation of your key.

24 Click evalToEnd to turn it back on, and drag the currentOp slider all the
way to the right.

25 Select Fine Tuning and scrub again on a green strand of hair.

26 Move the spillSponge slider all the way to the right.

The green spill is now under control.

Another useful Primatte function is the Status feature, which checks the values in your key. The Status output gives you a color code to determine where each of the pixels is positioned in the four Primatte zones:

27 Deactivate the Viewer DOD and fit the image to the Viewer.

28 Click the Output Status button.

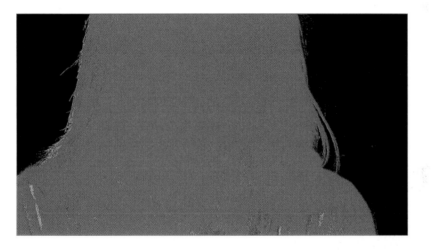

Primatte zones:

▶ Black, zone 1

   All background

▶ Blue, zone 2

   Transparent foreground

▶ Green, zone 3

   Suppressed foreground

▶ Red, zone 4

   All foreground

Compositing the Shot

The first part of this shot is almost done, but it needs some color correction and additional matte treatment. It would be best to complete the composite outside of Primatte. The output setting determines what is changed by Primatte:

▶   Alpha Only—Primatte affects only the matte.

▶   On Black—Primatte affects both the foreground image and the matte.

▶   Comp—If you have an optional second input image, this will composite the foreground with the background.

▶   Status—This special output gives you a color-coded image to determine where each of the pixels is positioned in the four Primatte zones.

1   Click the Alpha Only button.

Alpha Only will output an unaffected foreground along with its alpha channel. This will negate the spill suppression in the Primatte, but we will compensate for it later with color correction.

2 Click the dividing line between the Parameters workspace and the Node
workspace, and drag the line down to give yourself more room in the
Node workspace.

3 Click the Node View tab so that you can see your tree.

Matte Treatment

This shot's matte has some impurities in the background and is a bit ratty, so
you're going to work on it by using a DilateErode node.

1 Highlight the Primatte node.

2 From the Filter tab, add a DilateErode.

DilateErode isolates each channel and cuts pixels away or adds them to the
edge of the channel. It is good for either growing or shrinking mattes. For
example, if you wanted to eat into your matte, you would set your channels to *a* for the alpha channel and then set the Pixels to a value of *−1*. In
contrast, a positive value would grow the matte. By default, you are working with whole pixels, but you can switch to subpixel precision by toggling
on Soften. Note that the Soften parameter *really* slows the function down.
I recommend low values for the Pixel parameter if you are turning on the
Soften feature. When Soften is turned on, the Sharpness parameter controls how soft the edge is.

3 In the Channels parameter, delete *rgb* so that only the letter *a* shows.

DilateErode will now affect only the alpha channel.

4 View the alpha channel in the Viewer.

5 Set the Pixel parameter to a value of –2.

The DilateErode node has chewed into the matte slightly.

6 Activate Soften to turn on subpixel erosion of the edge.

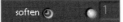

DilateErode removes some of the background impurities and shrinks the matte slightly. Next, you will composite the woman over the background.

7 Click the Proxy button and select P2.

8 View the RGB channels in the Viewer.

9 Add an Over node from the Layer tab and connect an output of bg to the right input.

10 Turn on preMultiply.

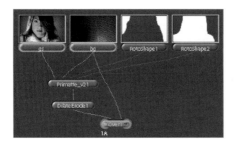

The composite is working pretty well so far except for the color balance of the woman in comparison with the background.

Color-Correcting the Shot

Try color-correcting the shot so that the woman's face is darker and bluer.

1   Highlight DilateErode1 in your tree.

2   From the Color tab, select a Mult and then a Brightness node.

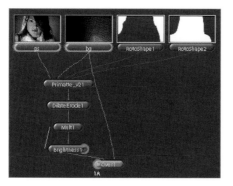

3   Set the Value parameter to *0.8.*

The brightness of the two elements matches.

4   Click the right side of the Mult1 node so that you can edit its parameters.

5   Expand the two Color subtrees and set red to *0.85,* green to *0.89,* and blue to *1.2.*

6   Click the Flipbook icon to check your progress.

The color match works for me now.

7   Close the flipbook when done.

8   Fit the image to the Viewer so that you can see the entire image.

Adding a Reflection

To finish the shot, let's add a reflection to the scene.

1   Make a flipbook of the reflection node.

Hold on a minute. The reflection has a camera move on it, which will need to be stabilized.

2   Set the proxyScale back to the Base setting by clicking the Proxy button on the top menu bar to check the composite at full resolution.

3   Highlight the **reflection** clip and select a Stabilize node from the Transform tab.

Be careful when placing the tracker. Pick a place on the frame where reflections aren't whizzing by.

4   Go to frame 58 and place the tracker over the top of the red thingy on the left side of the screen.

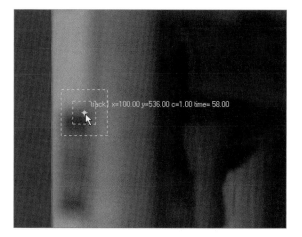

5   Turn limitProcessing on, which will make the tracking analysis go faster.

6 Click the reverse tracking button.

As the motion of the clip is analyzed, the screen turns black except for the area around the track, because limitProcessing is active.

7 When the tracker completes its motion analysis, turn on applyTransform.

8 Turn on the P2 proxy and create a flipbook.

The **reflection** clip is stabilized, but the stabilization has created a black border around the image. We can fix this by blowing the image up slightly with a Move2D node. Note that the greatest amount of black around the image occurs at frame 58.

9 Close the flipbook.

10 Go to frame 58 and add a Move2D node from the Transform tab after Stabilize1.

11 Use the onscreen controls to blow the image up enough to get rid of the black border; or just type in the parameters. I used the following settings:

Parameter	Value
xPixels	0
yPixels	−52
xScale	1.17
xScale	1.17

12 Click the Flipbook icon again, and you'll see that the black border is gone. Close the flipbook when you're done.

13 Drag the Time Bar to frame 18.

14 From theLayer tab, add a Screen node after Move2D1, and connect Over1 to the second input.

Are you sick of hearing that the Screen node is good for adding reflections? Too bad. I can tell you right now that the reflection is too bright. Use a Fade node to lower its intensity.

15 Highlight Move2D1 and select a Fade node from the Color tab.

Fade is similar to Brightness, but it also affects the alpha channel.

16 Set the Fade value to *0.5*.

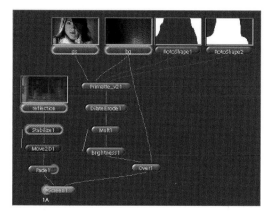

17 Make your last flipbook.

Everything looks good in motion. Check the composite one more time at full resolution.

18 Set the proxyScale back to the Base setting to return to full resolution.

19 Click the Home button beneath the Viewer to see the image at a 1:1 pixel ratio.

20 Look at the various portions of the image by dragging with the middle mouse button.

OK, that's it. Consider yourself a lean, mean keying machine.

21 Quit Shake.

Primatte Tips

▶ If you are having problems between the spill suppression, foreground, and background, move the Operator slider back to 0 and redo your initial Center pick. Click the color box and make a much smaller drag of the background area. This way, all subsequent operations will be much finer.

▶ Foreground and background scrubs can be as broad as you want. For the other color-picking parameters, including the initial Center scrub, short scrubs are recommended, even as fine as one pixel.

▶ You may need to pull several keys (for example, one key for the body, one for hair, another for clothing, and so on). Use Primatte's matte arithmetic settings to replace the foreground matte with the current Primatte matte, or add, subtract, or multiply the mattes.

▶ You can always leave the Primatte output on Alpha Only and adjust the matte further with other tools such as DilateErode, Blur, Gamma, and so on, and then apply a Mult afterwards.

▶ Primatte does its spill suppression by pulling in color from the background image. The reason for this is that if a person picked up blue spill from a blue field behind them, then they would probably also pick up red spill from a red brick wall. This means that the foreground sometimes will appear slightly transparent, even though the alpha channel is opaque. If you are having problems with this, use Primatte's replaceImage input. The replaceImage input allows you to use any image as the source for Primatte's color correction. Using a blurred version of the background in the replaceImage input is sometimes useful. Also, if a person is wearing a white shirt, you might want to set the replaceMode to use color and change the replaceColor to white.

Lesson Review

1. How many zones does Primatte use to map out color values?
2. Should scrubbing to select image values be broad or fine?
3. What does the spillSponge do?
4. Name a Viewer function that speeds up all image processes.

Answers

1. Primatte uses four zones to map out color values.
2. Foreground and background scrubs can be as broad as you want. For the other color-picking parameters, including the initial Center scrub, short scrubs as fine as one pixel are recommended.
3. The spillSponge removes color spill based on an initial scrub in the Viewer.
4. The Viewer DOD isolates an area and speeds up all image processes.

11

MultiPlane Compositing

The MultiPlane node is a compositing environment for positioning 2D layers within a 3D space. A virtual camera, similar to those found in 3D animation packages, controls the view of the output image. This camera can be animated by keyframing parameters or by importing 3D camera and tracking data from third-party programs. With these 3D tracking programs' exacting results, most of which are automatic, the MultiPlane node offers an efficient and increasingly popular alternative to traditional 2D compositing. Guess what? It also saves you loads of time.

FileIn the Source Material

1   Open Shake.

2   FileIn all the .iff files from the Lesson11 folder.

    You should have the following eight clips: car_mask, laser1, laser2,
    laser_reflection, logo, mercedes_comp, woman, and woman_roto.

    Take a moment to view the final composite before starting.

3   Find the mercedes_comp clip and load it into the Viewer.

4   On the Globals tab, set the timeRange to *1-70*.

5   Click the Home icon at the bottom-right of the interface to set the Time
    Bar range.

6   Click the Flipbook icon and play the clip once it is loaded.

    What you have here are your standard computer-generated laser beams
    and reflections added to a live-action background plate of a woman walk-
    ing in front of a sports car.

7   Repeat steps 3–6 to play the woman and laser clips.

8   Load the woman_roto and car_mask clips into flipbooks and play them.

The **car_mask** clip will appear black because it contains only an alpha channel.

9   Press the A key with your cursor over the **car_mask** flipbook to display its alpha channel.

10 Play the car_mask flipbook.

The **car_mask** and **woman_roto** clips will be used to isolate certain elements in the layering process.

11 Close all open flipbooks.

Preparing the Elements

A few of the elements need to be combined before they can be used in the MultiPlane node. To start, the **woman** and **car_mask** clips will be combined with a SwitchMatte node.

SwitchMatte copies a channel from the second image into the matte channel of the first image.

1   Highlight the **woman** clip and select a SwitchMatte node from the Layer tab.

2   Connect **car_mask** to the second input of SwitchMatte1.

When we get around to using the MultiPlane node, this element will allow you to place the lasers behind the car. The next element that needs isolating is the **woman** clip, so that the lasers can be positioned behind her as well. The RotoShape exercise you completed from Lesson 4 will come in handy right about now. If you completed Lesson 4 and rendered the **woman_roto** clip, you may load it instead of the version located in the Lesson11 folder.

3   Select the **woman** clip again, and Shift-click the SwitchMatte node in the Layer tab to create a new branch.

4   Connect the output of **woman_roto** to the second input of SwitchMatte2.

Taking a Tour of MultiPlane

The MultiPlane node has many capabilities, but its two primary uses are:

▶ To arrange multiple layers within a 3D space for easy simulation of perspective, parallax, and other depth effects.

▶ To composite background or foreground elements with a moving background using 3D camera tracking data, imported from a variety of third-party tracking software.

The MultiPlane node also provides transform controls such as panning, rotation, and scaling for each layer.

In this lesson, we will learn how to arrange multiple layers within a 3D space; in the next lesson, we will concentrate on importing 3D camera tracking data to composite elements over a moving background.

Using the Multiple Pane View

A multiple pane view is helpful when arranging layers in 3D space.

1 Highlight the **woman** clip, right-click the MultiPlane node from the Layer tab, and choose Branch.

The Viewer switches to a multipane interface.

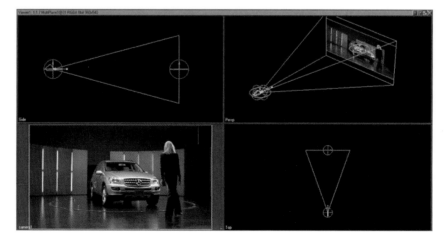

Each pane can be set to display any camera or angle in the 3D space, to help you position and transform objects from any angle.

2   Click the Viewer Layout button below the Viewer. Keep clicking to cycle through all the available layouts.

The size and orientation of each pane in all layouts are fixed, although you can zoom and pan within any pane using the standard methods.

3   Leave the Viewer layout on a single pane when done.

Changing Angles Within a Pane

Although the multipane layouts are fixed, you can change the angle each pane displays. The preset angles appear in white text at the bottom-left corner of each pane.

Persp

Each pane can display the currently selected camera, front, top, side, or perspective angle. So many choices, so little time.

You can change the displayed angle by doing one of the following:

▶   Right-click in a pane and select an angle from the shortcut menu, or

▶   Place your pointer in the pane you want to switch and press one of the numeric keypad keyboard shortcuts listed on the next page to switch layouts.

The following table lists the keyboard shortcuts that are available for changing angles in a pane. These shortcuts work only with the numeric keypad.

Keyboard Shortcuts

(Numeric keypad only)

0   cycles through every angle

1   displays the currently selected camera angle

2   displays the currently selected front angle

3   displays the currently selected top angle

4   displays the currently selected side angle

5   displays the currently selected perspective angle

The various angles are meant to help you position layers and the camera within 3D space. Each angle is actually an invisible camera.

Using the Perspective Angle

The perspective angle (Persp) is the only view in which you can transform a layer's X, Y, and Z parameters simultaneously. In addition to panning and zooming, the perspective angle can be orbited.

1   Set the single pane to the Persp view.

2   To orbit, click the pointer in the pane displaying the perspective view, press X, and drag with the middle mouse button held down.

      The perspective view rotates around the perspective's orbit point.

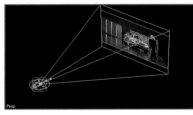 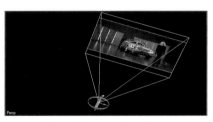

Default perspective view   Rotated perspective view

Are you dizzy yet?

3 To center the perspective on a selected object, place the cursor in the perspective view and press Shift-B.

The perspective view's orbit point is centered on the selected object, and the view is set to its default position.

Hardware Acceleration

The MultiPlane node supports the OpenGL hardware acceleration of images displayed in the Viewer. At the expense of rendering quality, Hardware rendering provides a quick way of positioning layers and the camera in space.

▶ Hardware mode doesn't provide an accurate representation of the final output, but it is the fastest method for arranging layers. In Hardware rendering mode, every layer is composited with an Over operation, regardless of that layer's selected composite type. Fast is good.

▶ Hardware/Software On Release mode sets the Viewer to use Hardware rendering while you're making adjustments, but it goes into Software rendering mode to show the image at its best quality. To turn this setting on, click and hold the Render Mode button and choose the icon below from the pop-up menu that appears.

▶ Software mode displays the selected camera at the highest quality with all composite types displayed properly.

The render mode affects only the display in the Viewer. The output of the MultiPlane node to other nodes in the tree is always at the highest quality, as are MultiPlane images that are rendered to disk.

Manipulating the Camera

The camera can be positioned or animated manually, like any other layer, or positioned and animated by importing 3D tracking or camera data from a Maya (.ma) file. Relax, you will import 3D tracking data in the next lesson.

Using 3D Transform Controls

1   Set the render mode to Hardware for faster interaction.

2   Press the spacebar while the cursor is in the Viewer to zoom it up to full-screen mode.

3   Press the F key with the cursor in the Viewer to fit the image.

4   Click the camera icon to display the image's 3D transform controls.

Camera   Camera target

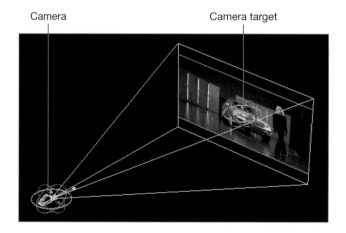

You can control the camera itself and the camera's target. The camera and target controls are connected so that they always face each other—moving one rotates the other to match its position.

5   Drag the camera.

Using Camera Controls

Similar to layer controls, the camera has rotate XYZ controls and translate (move) XYZ controls to limit the movement of the camera in one of those directions. Dragging the camera icon moves the camera within the Viewer.

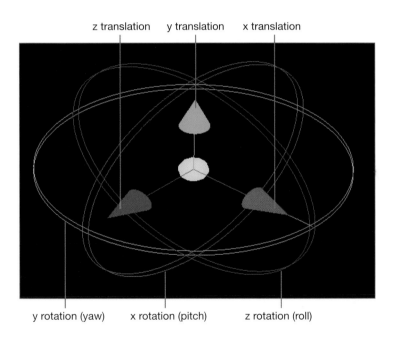

z translation   y translation   x translation

y rotation (yaw)   x rotation (pitch)   z rotation (roll)

1   Use the + key to zoom in to the camera.

2   Experiment with the onscreen controls.

3   When you're done playing around, right-click in the Viewer and choose
Camera1.

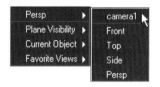

4   Press the F key with the cursor in the Viewer to fit the image to the Viewer.

A special group of keyboard shortcuts lets you move the camera by dragging anywhere within the camera view, without selecting the camera itself.

5   Try out the keyboard shortcuts listed below.

NOTE ▶ These keyboard shortcuts work only in the camera view.

Keyboard Shortcuts

V-drag	rotates the camera around its z-axis
S-drag	rotates the camera around the x- and y-axes, around the camera's own center point, changing the position of the camera target
Z-drag	pans the camera in and out along the z-axis
D-drag	pans the camera and camera target together along the x- and y-axes
X-drag	pivots the camera around the camera target's orbit point

Using Layer Controls

When you select a layer, that layer's onscreen controls are superimposed over it.

1   Click the **woman** image directly to select the layer.

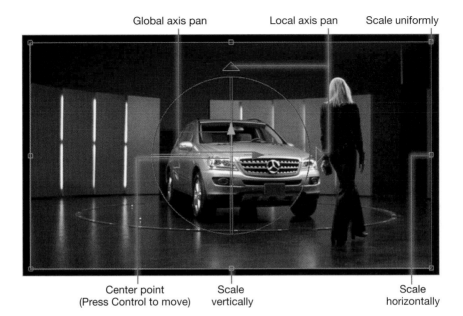

Global axis pan   Local axis pan   Scale uniformly

Center point   Scale   Scale
(Press Control to move)   vertically   horizontally

The global axis pan controls pan a layer relative to the overall 3D space, even if the layer has been rotated. The local axis pan controls pan the layer relative to its own orientation. If a layer has been rotated using the angle controls, using the local pan controls moves it along the axis of its own rotation.

2   Try both the local and global axis controls.

The following table shows Shake's dedicated keyboard shortcuts for panning, rotating, and scaling layers in 3D space, so you don't have to use the onscreen controls.

Keyboard Shortcuts

Q or P   pans

W or O   rotates

E or I   scales

The method for using any of these shortcuts is the same. Let's try W or O to rotate the layer.

3   Make sure the woman layer is still selected.

4   Press W or O and click in the Viewer.

5   When the dimension (multi-arrowed) pointer appears, move it in the direction in which you want to rotate the layer. The colors in the pointer correspond to the angle controls.

When you move the pointer, the axis in which you first moved is indicated by a single axis arrow, and the layer rotates in that dimension.

If you ever get tired of looking at the XYZ controls or if they get in your way, you can hide them by clicking the XYZ icon under the Viewer.

6   Press the spacebar to return the Viewer to normal size.

7   Right-click in the Parameters tab and choose Reset All Values.

8 Activate Hardware rendering mode for faster interaction.

Hooking Up the MultiPlane Node

Organize the nodes in the order of how you would like them hooked into the MultiPlane node. You can then attach all of these nodes to the single MultiPlane node simultaneously.

1 Organize the nodes from left to right in the following order: SwitchMatte1, SwitchMatte2, laser1, laser2, laser_reflection, and logo.

2 Drag across all of these nodes so that they are highlighted.

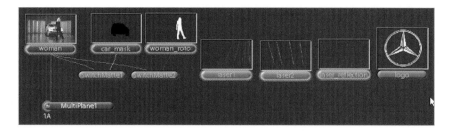

3 Shift-click the + input of the MultiPlane node.

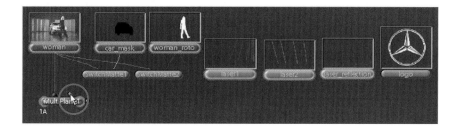

All selected nodes are connected to the MultiPlane node. By default, all new layers that you connect appear centered in the camera view.

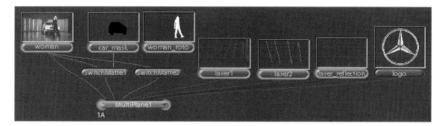

Creating the MultiPlane Composite

Once all of the images are connected to the MultiPlane node, the Viewer displays the multiple pane view below.

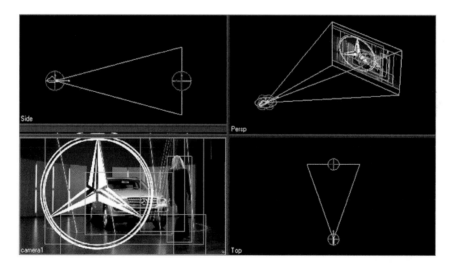

You can begin the composite by attaching layers to the camera.

Attaching Layers to the Camera

Attaching a layer to the camera locks the element to the camera perspective. As a result, the attached layer itself doesn't appear to move in the camera output, while any unattached layers that are positioned within the 3D workspace appear as if they're moving.

1   Click the Viewer Layout button on the Viewer toolbar until you are in single-pane view.

2   Press the F key to fit the image to the Viewer.

3   In the MultiPlane1 parameters, scroll down to the L1 (woman) layer, then click the Attach Layer to Camera button to lock this element to the camera perspective.

The woman layer is locked to the full area of the renderCamera angle in the Viewer.

4   Repeat step 3 for the rest of the layers, except for the logo layer, to lock them to the camera.

5   Scroll to the L7 (logo) layer and temporarily turn off its visibility. Don't worry, we will turn it on later.

The next step will be to set the filmGate in the Camera tab. The filmGate pop-up menu provides presets for setting the filmBack width and height parameters. There are options corresponding to most standard film formats.

6   Click the Camera tab.

7   Scroll down and set the filmGate to 35mm 1:85 Projection.

Placing Layers in 3D Space

The individual layers can now be properly placed in 3D space. Earlier, when you turned on the layers' Attach to Camera button, the faceCamera, parentTo, Pan, Angle, Scale, Center, and aspectRatio parameters all disappeared from those layers' subtrees in the Images tab, replaced by a single parameter—cameraDistance.

1   Go to frame 1 and expand the subtree beneath the L3 (**SwitchMatte2**) layer, and set the cameraDistance to *1250*.

The **woman** is now magically placed in front of the laser beams.

The cameraDistance parameter lets you adjust the spacing between layers attached to the camera, as well as between those layers and the other, unattached, layers and the other unattached layers that are arranged within the 3D workspace. This allows you to determine which layers appear in front of and behind attached layers.

2 Go to frame 27, expand the subtree for the L4 (laser1) layer, and set the cameraDistance to *1540*.

The laser1 layer is now positioned behind the car instead of in front of it.

3 Go to frame 30.

Do you see the laser reflections on the driver's side front wheel of the car? Well, you should have. *Thwack!* That was the sound of my hand swatting the back of your head.

4 Expand the subtree for the L6 (laser_reflection) layer and set the cameraDistance to *1540*.

Just like laser1, the laser_reflection layer is now positioned behind the car.

5 Right-click the image and switch to perspective view.

You should see that the layers are now placed at various distances in 3D space.

6 Press F to fit the image to the Viewer.

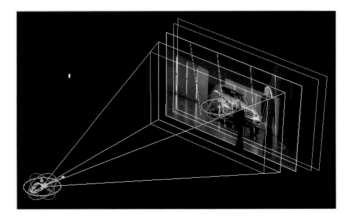

7   Preview your results by rendering a flipbook preview.

Not too shabby.

8   Close the flipbook and set your display back to the camera view by pressing the 1 key on the numeric keyboard.

9   Click the Viewer Layout button on the Viewer toolbar until you have a four-pane view.

10   Fit the camera image to the Viewer.

The last part of this lesson will show how an element can move through 3D space.

11   Go to frame 1 and turn on the visibility for the L7 (logo) layer.

12   Click the center of the Mercedes logo to activate its onscreen controls.

13   Drag it to the center of the screen.

14 Expand the subtree for the L7 (logo) layer and drag the Z pan parameter back and forth.

Watch how the logo layer changes layer priority in the 3D space in the various views. Oh, man, it's making me tingle.

15 Quit Shake.

Now that you have had a taste of the MultiPlane node, the next lesson will explore it in greater depth. You'll import 3D tracking data and use it to add computer-generated elements to the scene.

Lesson Review

1. What are the four views of the MultiPlane node?
2. Which render mode is the most efficient?
3. How can you quickly hook up all inputs of the MultiPlane node?
4. Describe the purpose of the cameraDistance parameter.

Answers

1. Camera, top, side, and perspective.
2. The Hardware setting is the most efficient render mode.
3. Highlight the nodes and Shift-click the plus sign (+) input of the MultiPlane node.
4. The cameraDistance parameter lets you adjust the relative spacing between layers that are attached to the camera, and between those layers and the unattached layers in the workspace.

Keyboard Shortcuts

Multipane View

(numeric keypad only)

0	cycles through every angle
1	displays the camera angle
2	displays the front angle
3	displays the top angle
4	displays the side angle
5	displays the perspective angle

Perspective View

Shift-B	centers the Perspective view on a selected object

Camera View

V-drag	rotates the camera around its z-axis
S-drag	rotates the camera around the x- and y-axes, around the camera's own center point, changing the position of the camera target
Z-drag	pans the camera in and out along the z-axis
D-drag	pans the camera and camera target together along the x- and y-axes
X-drag	pivots the camera around the camera target's orbit point

MultiPlane Transform

Q or P	pans
W or O	rotates
E or I	scales

12

Lesson Files
APTS_Shake > Lessons > Lesson12

Media
camera_file.ma

coke_comp.1-109#.iff

frame.1-109#.iff

neon.0001.iff

trailer.1-109#.iff

Time
This lesson takes approximately 2 hours to complete.

Goals
Use 3D tracking data in the MultiPlane node

Create a Glow macro

Use the Curve Editor to modify an animation

Animate with local variables and expressions

Transfer the animation of other nodes with parameter linking

Advanced Compositing

In this lesson, you will integrate computer-generated elements with a live-action background by importing and massaging 3D tracking data. Then you'll produce the finished shot by creating a macro and using advanced animation tools such as parameter linkings, local variables, and expressions. Animation is traditionally known as creating imagery on a frame-by-frame basis either by hand or digitally with computers. In this lesson, you will be using tools and techniques that will save the labor of animating on every single frame.

FileIn the Source Material

1   Open Shake.

2   FileIn the **coke_comp.1-109#.iff**, **frame.1-109#.iff**, **neon.0001.iff**, and **trailer.1-109#.iff** files from the Lesson12 folder.

View the final composite.

3   Find the **coke_comp** clip and load it into the Viewer.

4   In the Globals tab, set the timeRange to *1-109*.

5   Click the Flipbook icon and play the clip once it is loaded.

The neon sign and its reflection were added to the moving shot of the trailer.

6 Repeat the previous steps to play the **trailer** and **frame** clips.

7 Double-click the **neon** clip to load it into the Viewer.

These are your elements. The one-frame **neon** sign clip will have to be tracked onto the **trailer** background plate, while the **frame** clip will act as a minor reflective element for the sign.

8 Close all open flipbooks.

Before you assemble all these elements into a MultiPlane node with imported 3D tracking data, they will need to be prepped. To start with, you will want to create a glow for the neon sign. Because a glow effect is something that you could use on more than one occasion, you will create a reusable glow macro.

Creating a Macro

So what is a macro for, anyway? With macros, you can combine common functions into a new function that can be used to humiliate your friends and impress your enemies. You can control what parameters are exposed, and hide the ones that don't need changing. Macros are extremely powerful ways of modifying functions to suit your own needs. In this lesson, you'll build a spiffy macro that allows you to create glows around highlights that mimic photographic auras.

Creating Macros with the MacroMaker

The MacroMaker is an interactive tool to help you create new nodes by recombining previously existing nodes. Shake's scripting language is basically C-like, meaning you have access to an entire programming language to manipulate your scripts. Because the MacroMaker can't account for all possibilities, you should think of it as a tool for helping you get started in using Shake's language: Use the MacroMaker to build the initial files, and then modify those files to customize your macros.

> **NOTE** ▶ If you need to open the premade script for this lesson, you must first complete the macro exercise for the script to function properly.

Building the Glow Tree

Before the macro can be made, we must first build the Glow tree.

1   Highlight the **neon** clip and select a LumaKey node from the Key tab.

As you recall from earlier lessons, LumaKey creates a key in the alpha channels based on overall luminance. It will be used here to isolate the highlights from the neon sign.

2   Activate the matteMult parameter.

3   Add a Blur node from the Filter tab and set the Pixels parameter to *40*.

4   Select a Brightness node from the Color tab and set the value to *1.2*.

5   From the Layer tab, insert a Screen function.

The Screen function mimics the effect of exposing two film negatives together. It's particularly handy for reflections and luminescent elements, as it preserves the highlights.

6   Connect another output from the **neon** clip to the second input of Screen1.

We have achieved glow.

Now that you have something that would be a pain in the neck to re-create, it seems like a good idea to make a macro.

7   Drag over all the nodes except the neon node.

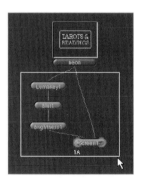

8   Click Shift-M (or, using the right mouse menu, Macro > MakeMacro).

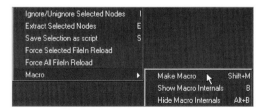

This will bring up the MacroMaker.

Creating the Macro

The top part of the window allows you to enter the name of the macro and the tab it will go in. By default, the macro is called UserMacro, and it will create a new tab called User.

1 Change the Macro Name to *Glow* and press Enter.

The next line tells Shake where to store the macro. "User directory" means your local user directory. Macros stored here will be available to you only on the local machine.

2 Make sure "User directory" is selected.

"Shake directory" means in your *ShakeDirectory*/include/startup directory. This will be available to everybody who opens Shake using that specific version in that specific directory. "Macro's output is" tells you what node is going to be spit out of the new macro. Shake usually makes a good guess on this, but you may need to specify it explicitly if you have selected multiple branches. In this example, Screen1 is the proper output.

The next box contains the list of parameters you want to add, the names you want to give the variables, and the default values you want to supply.

Let's go through the various nodes and change some of the values.

3   Expand the Blur1 parameters and do the following: Change the Float xPixels parameter name to *glowSize* and the default value to *20*, and make sure the Visibility button is on.

4   Expand the Brightness1 parameters and do the following: Change the Float Value parameter name to *glowBrightness* and the default value to *1*, and make sure the Visibility button is on.

5 Expand the LumaKey1 parameters and do the following: Change the Float loVal parameter name to *glowLowVal* and the Float hiVal parameter name to *glowHiVal*, and make sure the Visibility buttons are on.

6 Click OK when you're ready. You should have a new tab named User with a button called Glow in it.

Test the Macro

1 Delete all nodes connected to the **neon** clip.

2 Right-click the Glow icon on the User tab and choose Create.

3 Connect the **neon** clip to both inputs of Glow1.

   You should see four controls in the Parameter workspace.

4 Adjust the various parameters to see their effect.

   If you want to see the guts of Glow, you can expand the internal nodes that make up the macro.

5   Highlight Glow1, right-click Node View, and choose Macro > Show Macro
Internals.

6   Drag the corners of the window to make it larger, and use the mouse buttons to reposition the nodes so that you can see them.

The nodes that make up the macro appear in the form of a tree.

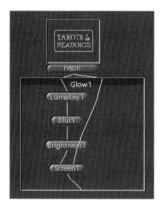

7   Close the macro window by clicking the minimize button at top right.

How to Add an Icon to the Interface

Now, I'll show you how to create a button in the user interface and attach a function to it. We're going to use the output of Glow1 to build ourselves an icon. The icons for the tabs have three qualities:

▶ They measure 75x40 pixels.

▶ They have no alpha channel.

▶ They are saved in your icons directory as *TabName.Name*.nri.

Let's get started.

1 Select Color from the Image tab and set the Res parameters to *75x40*.

 The Color node sets the resolution.

2 Select an AddText node from the Layer tab.

3 Set the fontScale to *30*, type *Glow* in the text field, and press Enter.

4 Change the second position parameter to *25*.

5 Add Glow from the User tab after AddText1.

6 Connect AddText1 to both inputs of Glow2.

7 Set the glowSize to *25* and the glowBrightness to *2*.

 It's looking good.

The alpha channel should be removed, so let's add a SetAlpha node.

8   On the Color tab, add a SetAlpha node after Glow2 and set the alpha parameter to *0*.

That's it. Just render it using a FileOut node from the Image tab.

9   Select SetAlpha1 and insert a FileOut node.

10   When the File Browser comes up, create an icon directory in *UserDirectory*/nreal (if you don't already have one) by using the Create Folder button in the File Browser.

11   Type *icons* for the folder name and click OK.

12   Save the image as User.Glow.nri (*TabName.MacroName*.nri) in the icon directory you just created.

The .nri extension stands for Nothing Real icon. (Nothing Real was the company that originally created Shake.)

13   Right-click the FileOut node you just created and choose Render > Render FileOut Nodes from the pop-up menu.

14   When the Render Parameters window opens, set the timeRange to *1* and click Render.

We now have the two elements that we need: the macro and the icon. We now want to place the icon into the interface. To do that, quit Shake so that you can make the necessary user interface code modifications.

15   Quit Shake.

16   Open the TextEdit program, located in the Applications folder.

17   Choose File > Open and go to your *UserDirectory*/nreal/include/ startup/ui directory.

18 Double-click GlowUI.h.

The GlowUI.h file looks like this:

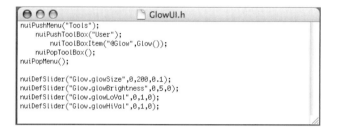

```
nuiPushMenu("Tools");
    nuiPushToolBox("User");
        nuiToolBoxItem("@Glow",Glow());
    nuiPopToolBox();
nuiPopMenu();

nuiDefSlider("Glow.glowSize",0,200,0.1);
nuiDefSlider("Glow.glowBrightness",0,5,0);
nuiDefSlider("Glow.glowLoVal",0,1,0);
nuiDefSlider("Glow.glowHiVal",0,1,0);
```

The second line tells what tab the macro will go into—in this case the User tab. The third line adds the function. The first occurrence of *Glow* is calling the icon file that we just created. It assumes you have matched the tab name with the filename. The next occurrence of *Glow* is the actual function, followed by its default values.

The @ before *Glow* on the third line is used if you don't want an icon; it is the default behavior when using the MacroMaker. All we need to do is remove the @, and your new icon will show up in the interface.

19 On the third line, remove the @ before *Glow* and save the file.

20 Open Shake and go to the User tab.

You will no doubt see your new icon:

Wipe that silly grin off your face.

Create a Flickering Neon Light

Now you're going to take the static **neon** image and turn it into a nice, soft flickering sign.

1 FileIn the **frame.1-109#.iff**, **neon.0001.iff**, and **trailer.1-109#.iff** files once again from the Lesson12 folder.

2   On the Globals tab, set the timeRange to *1-109*.

3   Click the Home icon at the bottom right of the interface to sync the Time Bar to the Globals timeRange.

4   Right-click the Glow icon in the User tab and choose Create.

5   Connect **neon** clip to both inputs of Glow1.

6   Set the glowSize to *40* and the glowBrightness to *1.2*.

The neon sign would look better if you increased its saturation.

7   From the Color tab, add a Saturation node and set it to *1.75*.

The glow now looks pretty good, but the neon sign really needs to flicker, as all neon signs should.

8   Add a Blur node from the Filter tab and a Brightness node from the Color tab.

You're going to manually animate the Brightness and Blur parameters to create a soft flickering light, which will be sure to strain your mouse finger. Later in the lesson, you'll learn how to accomplish the same result by inserting an expression into Brightness1's Value parameter.

9   Go to frame 1 and click the Keyframe toggle next to the Value parameter.

10 Enter *0.91* for the value.

11 At frame 3, enter *0.2*.

12 Go to frame 8 and enter *0.91*.

The Curve Editor

While you've been setting keyframes, these values are simultaneously being entered as curves in the Curve Editor. Follow these steps to see what the curve looks like numerically:

1   Click the + to the left of the Value parameter.

Are you feeling both confused and impressed at the same time? Suppose I told you that you're looking at a numeric representation of the keyframes that have been set. It makes more sense now, right?

The Curve Editor allows you to see a visual representation of animated keyframes on a graph. You are able to create, see, and modify these animation curves. When you activated keyframing, the Clock icon next to the parameter was also activated. When a checkmark is on the Clock icon, it will be loaded into the Curve Editor.

2   Make sure that the Value parameter's Clock icon has a checkmark next to it.

3   Select the Curve Editor in the tool tabs.

The Curve Editor displays the animation curve for the Value parameter of Brightness1.

4   Click the Home icon below the Curve Editor to center the curve.

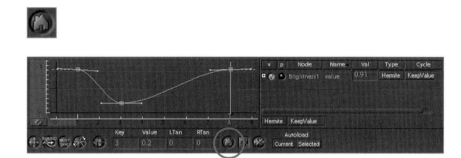

Take a deep breath and enjoy the beauty of the curve. All right, that's enough, snap out of it.

Adding and Deleting Keys

You can add keyframes on the curve by Shift-clicking it.

1   Shift-click the curve between frames 3 and 8, and a keyframe will be created.

You can drag it around, or, if it is still selected, you can enter numerical values in the text fields at the bottom of the Curve Editor.

You can delete keyframes in two ways:

▶   Drag a selection box around the keyframe or keyframes and press the Delete key on the keyboard.

▶   Move the Time Bar to where the key is and click the Delete Keyframe button if you are using an onscreen control.

2   Drag a selection box around the keyframe that you added and press the
Delete key on the keyboard.

Selecting Keyframes and Curves

You can select curves and keyframes in several ways:

▶   Drag the mouse over a segment to select a curve, or Shift-drag to add to a
selection.

▶   Drag over keyframes to select them.

▶   Press Command-A to select all curves.

▶   Press Shift-A to select all points on active curves.

▶   Use the Curve List to select curves by name.

Modifying Values

You can modify a value by:

▶   Grabbing keyframes and adjusting their position in the Curve Editor.

▶   Changing a keyframe's value in the Parameters workspace or onscreen
controls when AutoKey is turned on.

▶   Selecting the keyframe and using the text ports at the bottom of the screen
as virtual sliders (Control-drag) to change the Key (its time) or Value
entries.

1   Drag a selection box over the keyframe at frame 3 to select it.

2 In the Value text box, change the value from .2 to *.86* and press Enter.

3 Set the following keyframe values in the Parameter workspace:

Frame	Value
2	.79
4	.80
5	.97
6	.88
7	.77

4 Right-click in the Curve Editor and choose View > Frame Selected.

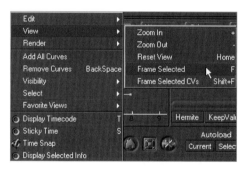

The curve is framed within the Curve Editor.

NOTE ▶ See the end of this lesson for a complete list of Curve Editor keyboard shortcuts. For detailed information on the Curve Editor, please refer to the Shake User Manual.

Setting the Cycle Mode

1 Drag the Time Bar back and forth between frames 1 and 8.

The curve you created works fine as an animation for the flickering of the neon sign, but it's too short. The Curve Editor has a number of Cycle modes, one of which can cycle the animation. Let's try it out.

2 Click the KeepValue tab below Cycle and choose RepeatValue from the pop-up menu.

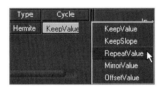

3 Press Control-Alt and drag to the left in the Curve Editor to expand the displayed frame range.

The eight-frame animation now continuously repeats, courtesy of RepeatValue.

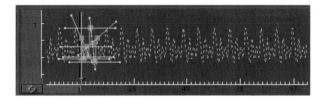

4 Click the Flipbook icon and play what you have done so far.

The neon sign flickers randomly—not bad for setting only eight keyframes.

5 Close the flipbook.

Animation Using Expressions

The cycle animation you created was the equivalent of starting a fire with flint and steel. It's time to break out the blowtorch.

1 Right-click the Brightness1 Parameter tab and choose Reset All Values.

2 Click in the Value text field and replace the number 1 with the word *time*.

This uses the current frame number for the Value parameter.

3 Move the Time Bar to various frames.

This brightens the image as you get to higher frames, since at frame 109 it creates a brightness value of 109.

4 Click the + next to the Value parameter.

You will see an expanded text field with your expression—time—in it. The normal text field shows you the result of that expression at that frame. You can put any expression here, so let's do something clever like using a random function.

5 Type *rnd(time)*.

This will return a random value between 0 and 1, with time as your variable. The rnd function isn't truly random, but by using time as the variable, you guarantee that the values will differ from frame to frame.

6   Click the Flipbook icon to preview the animation and close it when you're done.

> **NOTE** ▶ If you move the slider on the Value parameter by mistake, you will remove the expression. To get it back, simply retype the expression, or click Undo (if using the full version of Shake). The only exception to this behavior is if your expression is an animated curve that you create with keyframes.

7   To see the animated values in the Curve Editor, click the Clock icon next to Value and open the Curve Editor.

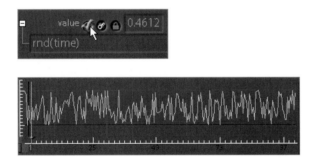

Your dreams of impressing those around you with your mastery of expressions will no doubt be destroyed when you try clicking the erratic curve. Nothing happens. Why? Because you aren't using keyframe animation. So read on to see how you control an expression.

8   Right-click Brightness1's Parameter1 tab. From the pop-up menu, choose Create Local Variable.

This means you will be adding an extra parameter to Brightness1 with which you can do whatever you want. A window will appear prompting you to name your local variable and select its type. A variable can be one of the following types:

▶ Float—A number with a decimal place (0.1, 0.5, 1.0, and so on)

▶ String—Characters ("The quick brown fox …")

▶ Int—A rounded number (0, 1, 2, and so on)

9 In the Variable Name field, type *rndVal*, keep the Variable Type as Float, and click OK.

A new subtree named localParameters will appear in Brightness1's parameters.

If you adjust the slider, you will see that absolutely nothing happens. Be patient. First add another local variable and more expressions.

10 Right-click the Parameter1 tab again and choose Create Local Variable.

11 Name it *animVal* and keep it on Float.

It would be pretty impressive if you could set some keyframes in the animVal local variable that would control the random time animation. Give it a try.

12 Go to frame 1, turn on the AutoKey for animVal, and set three keyframes. Enter values of *0.5* at frame 1, *0.4* at frame 55, and *0.6* at frame 109.

13 Click the Home button below the Curve Editor to show all your curves.

This centers all your curves within the Curve Editor, but the animVal keyframes are not controlling the random time animation. To do this, you first have to move the rnd(time) expression from Value to rndVal and then write a new expression for Value.

14 Click the word *value* (a little hand holding a piece of paper should appear), drag down to rndVal, and release the mouse button.

15 Open rndVal's subtree.

You should see rnd(time) as its new expression.

16 Open Value's subtree, double-click Value's expression, and replace it with *rndVal*animVal*.

This will multiply the results of rndVal and animVal together.

17 Make sure Value and animVal—but not rndVal—are loaded in the Curve Editor.

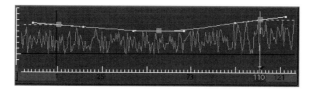

Finally, you can see that the curve is modifying the shape of the otherwise random curve.

18 Go ahead and grab the keyframes or insert a new one. When you do, you change the form of the random shape.

19 Drag the Time Bar to various frames to get an idea of what the animation looks like.

Now that you can control the random flickering, you can link the animation in Brightness1's Value parameter to Blur1's xPixels. This will give the blur the same random animation as in Brightness1's Value parameter.

20 Click the right side of the Blur1 node to edit its parameters.

21 Open the Pixels subtree, click in the xPixels text field, and type *Brightness1.value*75.*

The *75 is for multiplying the result of Brightness1's Value animation, which is in a range of only 0.4 to 0.6. Multiplying by 75 makes the effect of the blur noticeable.

22 Drag the Time Bar again to see what is happening.

The blur randomly animates along with the flickering neon through parameter linking. Our last step will be to combine this random flicker animation with the original neon element.

23 Highlight the Saturation1 node, right-click IAdd from the Layer tab, and choose Branch.

24 Connect the output of Brightness1 to the second input of IAdd1.

25 Set the IAdd percent parameter to *50*.

26 Press Control-E over the tree to activate Enhanced Node View.

Your tree should look like this:

In Enhanced Node View, a purple line connecting Blur1 to Brightness1 signifies that an expression exists between them.

27 Double-click the IAdd1 node, make a flipbook, and play it.

The **neon** element is now complete and ready for the MultiPlane node.

28 Close your flipbook.

Highlighting the Metal Frame

The neon sign element will ultimately fit inside the trailer's metal frame. The **frame** clip, which already matches the motion of the trailer, was generated to provide a green glow around this metal frame.

1 Select the **trailer** clip and choose an IAdd node from the Layer tab.

2 Connect the frame image to the second input of IAdd2.

3 Go to frame 109 so you can see the frame.

4 Place your pointer over the IAdd2 node and press I repeatedly to toggle the effect on and off.

The frame looks harsh around the edges and could use a bit of softening.

5 Make sure that the IAdd2 node is in the active state.

6 From the Filter tab, insert a Blur node between the frame and IAdd2 nodes.

7   Set the Pixels to a value of 6.

That does the trick.

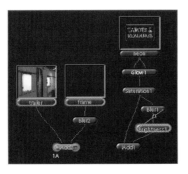

8   Make a flipbook and play it.

All elements are prepped, and it's time to import camera-tracking data into the MultiPlane node to create the proper perspective change for the 2D images.

MultiPlane and 3D Tracking Data

The MultiPlane node supports .ma (Maya ASCII) files, allowing you to import 3D camera paths or use 3D tracking data clouds generated by third-party tracking applications. The imported tracking data can be used to match-move elements within the MultiPlane node.

> **NOTE ▶** The MultiPlane node automatically puts layers within your camera view so you can find them easily. However, if you attach layers after applying the camera or tracking data, you may find the newly attached layers with unexpected offsets.

Connecting the Elements

1   Rename IAdd2 as *trailer_comp* and IAdd1 as *neon_comp*.

2   Right-click a MultiPlane node from the Layer tab and choose Create.

3   Connect trailer_comp first and then neon_comp twice to the MultiPlane node.

Two copies of neon_comp are used because one of them will serve as
a reflection element.

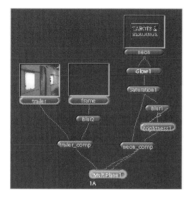

Importing the 3D Tracking Data

The **trailer_comp** clip has a camera dolly move with noticeable changes in perspective. The **neon_comp** clip is a static sign with an animated glow, which
must be matched to the trailer's camera move. Only **neon_comp** will make use
of the MultiPlane camera move. Since **trailer_comp** already has a camera move,
you will need to lock it to the camera view to avoid a perspective change.

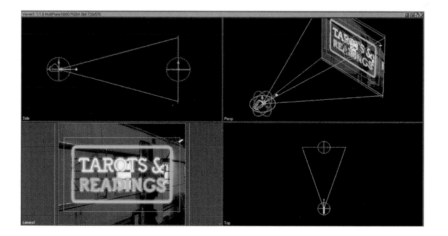

1 With the pointer over the camera1 view, press F to fit the image to the
Viewer.

2 To start with, activate the Hardware rendering mode for faster interaction.

3 In the MultiPlane1 parameters, click the Camera tab.

4 Click the Load button at the bottom of the Camera tab.

5 In the File Browser, navigate to the Lesson12 folder, then select the **camera.ma** file and click OK.

The point cloud data appears. A point cloud is a series of tracked points that follow along with features in the image.

Every new MultiPlane node is created with one camera, named camera1. Importing an .ma file adds a camera to the renderCamera pop-up menu in the Camera tab of the MultiPlane node's parameters.

6   Go back to the Images tab.

I can't stand it anymore! The points in the cloud are so large, my head is going to explode.

7   Go to the Globals tab, open the guiControls subtree, and adjust the multiPlaneLocatorScale to *0.2*.

Thank you.

8   Go back to the Parameters1 tab.

Attaching Layers to the Tracking Data

Attaching the layer that produced the tracking data to the camera forces the attached layer to follow along with the camera as it moves according to the tracking data. As a result, the attached layer itself doesn't appear to be moving in the camera output, while the unattached layers that are positioned within the 3D workspace appear as if they're moving along with the features in the attached layer.

1 Scroll down to the L1 (trailer_comp) layer, and then click the Attach Layer to Camera button to lock this element to the camera perspective.

To make the composite as real as possible, a reflection of the neon sign should be added to the trailer. Because L2 will be used as the reflection element, it should be parented to L3. Any adjustments to L3 will cascade down to L2.

2 Open the L2 subtree.

3 Change the L2_parentTo parameter to L3.

Wherever L3 moves, L2 will follow.

In addition to attaching layers to the camera, you can also attach a layer to any locator point in the data cloud. This lets you quickly set a layer's position in space to match that of a specific feature in a tracked background plate. In this case, you should attach one of the locator points to L3 (neon_comp).

4   Go to frame 109.

There's a point in the middle of the metal frame.

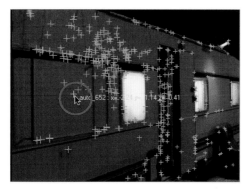

5   Right-click the point and choose L3 (neon_comp) from the Attach Plane menu.

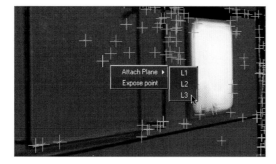

Layer 3 and Layer 2 (because it is parented to L3) both have the tracking data applied to them.

Massaging the Tracking Data

Sometimes the tracking data isn't completely accurate because of factors such as lens distortion. In that case, you will need to set some extra keyframes to have an accurate track. Before the accuracy of the track can be determined, the rotation and scale of L3 (neon_comp) need adjusting so that it properly fits within the metal frame.

1   Make sure that you are still at frame 109.

2   Open the L3 (neon_comp) subtree.

3   Set the L3_scale X and Y parameters to *0.0884* and *0.1297*, respectively.

4   Zoom in to the top view of the point cloud.

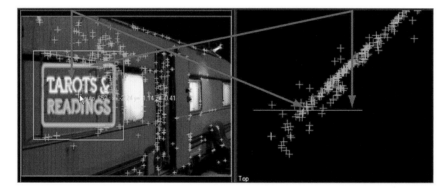

5   Hover over the locator point that you attached to L3.

The locator becomes highlighted in both the camera and top views. Note that the horizontal line in the top view represents L3. It should be rotated to be on the same plane as the point cloud to maintain the same perspective as the tracked points.

6   Control-drag in the L3_angle Y parameter (the center parameter) until the
layer lines up with the point cloud. I came up with a value of 43.9.

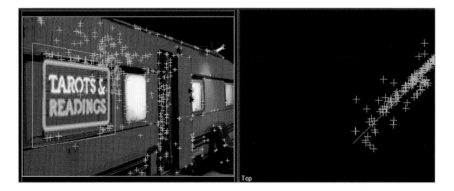

7   Click the Point Cloud Display button to disable it. We no longer need to
look at those stinking points.

The Z rotation is slightly off.

8   Adjust the L3_angle Z parameter (the far right parameter) until the sign
lines up with the frame. A value of 0.7 worked for me.

9   Make a flipbook to see how the tracking looks.

All in all, the neon sign is locked to the trailer image, except for some horizontal sliding. At frame 20, the neon is to the right of the frame. At frame
80, the neon fits perfectly within the frame. If a couple of keyframes are
set, the neon sign will be completely locked. Normally, you would think
of using the pan parameters to fix the horizontal sliding. Since the pan
parameters are taken over by the tracking data, the center controls can be
used instead to make the necessary corrections.

10 Click the Viewer Layout button below the Viewer until you have a single pane.

11 Go to frame 80 and open the L3_center subtree.

12 Right-click the L3_xCenter numeric field and choose Clear Expression from the pop-up menu.

13 Activate keyframing for the L3_xCenter parameter.

When the Keyframe toggle is activated, an xCenter keyframe is set at the current value. This sets the end position for the tracking correction.

14 Go to frame 20 and Control-drag in the L3_xCenter field until the neon is just to the left of the frame. A value of 382.2 is good.

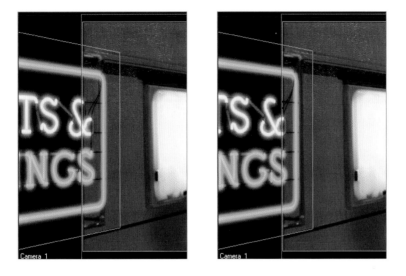

15 Make another flipbook to check the tracking.

Tracking looks good.

Making the Reflection

In the last part of the lesson, we'll cast a reflection of the neon sign onto the trailer.

1 Go to frame 80.

2 Open the L2 subtree and scroll to the L2_pan and L2_scale parameters.

3 Set the L2_pan X to −83 and L2_scale Y to 0.9.

The positioning of the reflection looks OK. Let's just add some blur and fade it out a touch.

4 Highlight neon_comp and Shift-click Blur in the Filter tab to create a new branch.

5 Set Pixels to 40.

6 Select a Fade node on the Color tab and set it to 0.5.

7 Connect Fade1 to the L2 or middle input of the MultiPlane1 node.

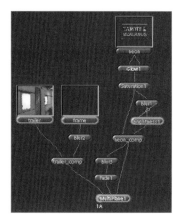

8 Double-click the MultiPlane1 node and make a flipbook.

At frame 109, the reflection is spilling over the left vertical frame bar. This bugs me, because it isn't right.

To fix this minor problem, we'll use an Outside node with a rotoshape to knock a hole into the reflection element.

9   Select a RotoShape node from the Image tab.

10   Highlight Fade1 and, from the Layer tab, add an Outside function.

Remember, the Outside node cuts a hole in the first image based on the alpha channel from the second image.

11   Connect the output of RotoShape1 to the second input of Outside1.

12   Make sure you are on frame 109.

13 Click the left side of MultiPlane1 to edit its parameters, and click the right side of RotoShape1.

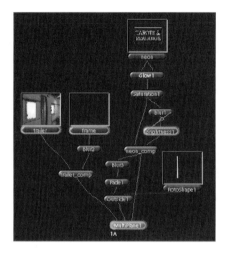

14 Set the Res parameters to 720x576.

15 Draw a shape around the left vertical frame bar.

This knocks out the reflection from the left side of the frame.

16 Make one last flipbook.

That's all she wrote. Congratulations!

17 Quit Shake.

Lesson Review

1. What is a macro?

2. Which Curve Editor Cycle mode continuously cycles the selected keyframes?

3. What type of camera or 3D tracking file can the MultiPlane node import?

4. What MultiPlane parameter locks the layer to the camera perspective?

Answers

1. A macro is the combination of commonly used functions in a new function.

2. The RepeatValue Cycle mode continuously cycles the selected keyframes.

3. The MultiPlane node supports .ma (Maya ASCII) files, allowing you to import 3D camera paths or use 3D tracking data clouds.

4. The Attach Layer to Camera button locks a layer to the camera perspective.

Keyboard Shortcuts

Curve Editor

Option-drag	pans window
Control-Option-drag	zooms window
+/= (by the Delete key)	zooms in and out
Option-drag on numbered axis	pans only in that direction
drag on numbered axis	scales in that direction
S	syncs the time to the current keyframe
T	toggles the timecode/frame display
Shift-drag	selects keyframes
Control-drag	deselects keyframes
Command-A	selects all curves
Shift-A	selects all knots on the active curve
Control-click tangent	breaks the tangent
Shift-click tangent	rejoins broken tangents
Q	moves selected points

Keyboard Shortcuts

Curve Editor *(continued)*

W	scales points; this is a two-step process: you first click the scale center, and then a second point to pull toward or away from the first point you clicked
X/Y	allows movement on only the *x*- or *y*-axis; pressing the key again frees that axis
H	flattens keyframe tangents
V	toggles the visibility of the selected curves
K	inserts a keyframe on the current cursor position on the curve
Del	deletes active keys
Delete	removes curves from the Curve Editor (does not delete them)
F, Control-F	frames selected curves
Shift-F	frames selected knots
Home	frames all curves

13

Lesson Files   APTS_Shake > Lessons > Lesson13

Media   cadillac_comp.1-64.iff

car.1-64.iff

scarf.1-64.iff

Time   This lesson takes approximately 1 hour to complete.

Goals   Composite using a stabilize/destabilize technique

Create a key using the Keylight keyer

Use the Warper to deform an image

Lesson 13
Warping

Warping is a process that deforms a portion of an image. The warp effect can be animated over time or done as a static adjustment that occurs over the entire shot. It can be used to make animals talk, enhance facial expressions, or cause body parts to shrink or expand. I am not saying one more word.

You'll use Shake's Warper node to adjust the shape of this woman's scarf.

FileIn the Source Material

1   Open Shake.

2   FileIn the **cadillac_comp.1-64.iff**, **car.1-64.iff**, and **scarf.1-64.iff** files from the Lesson13 folder.

    View the final composite before starting.

3   Load the **cadillac_comp** clip into the Viewer.

4   On the Globals tab, set the timeRange to *1-64*.

5   Click the Home icon at the bottom-right of the interface to set the Time Bar range.

6   Click the Flipbook icon and play the clip once it is loaded.

The scarf, photographed against a green screen, has been extracted and composited into the scene.

7   Load the **scarf** clip into a flipbook.

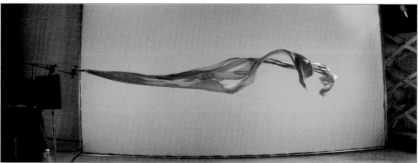

The scarf is your green screen element, which will be warped, positioned, and keyed over the car background plate.

8   Make a flipbook of the **car** clip.

The car background plate has camera motion, which will either need to be stabilized or applied to any elements added to it.

9   Close all open flipbooks.

The Old Stabilize/Destabilize Trick

When you are adding elements to a moving image, you essentially have two choices. First, you could analyze the motion of the moving clip and apply that motion to your elements. Or you could stabilize the moving clip, combine all of your elements, and then destabilize the composite. This second method restores the original motion to the finished shot.

1   Highlight the **car** clip and select a Stabilize node from the Transform tab.

2   Go to frame 1 and place the tracker over the rear headrest.

3   Size the reference pattern around the dark areas of the headrest.

If the reference pattern is too large, the tracker will wander during the analysis process.

4   Turn limitProcessing on, which will make the tracking analysis go faster.

5   Click the forward tracking button.

As the motion of the clip is analyzed, the screen turns black except for the area around the tracker, because limitProcessing is active.

6   When the tracker completes its motion analysis, turn on applyTransform.

7   Create a flipbook.

The black border that moves around the edges of the image is a dead give-away that the car image has been stabilized. You are now ready to composite.

8   Close the flipbook.

Key the Scarf

Your next step is to key the scarf image over the car using the Keylight keyer, developed by Framestore CFC in London. Keylight is the queen—come on, it's from London—of one-click keyers. With a one-click keyer, very little work is required to obtain a good result if the footage was shot properly.

1   Drag the Time Bar to frame 48.

2   In the Node View, select the scarf node and add a Keylight node from the Key tab.

3   Connect the output of Stabilize1 to the second input (the background input) of the Keylight node.

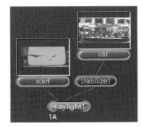

Let's set the color space you will be working in.

4   For this composite, set the Colourspace mode to Video.

Keylight has several color controls; right now we are concerned only with screenColour.

5   Click the screenColour color swatch (the blue box).

6   Drag your pointer across an area of the green screen in the Viewer.

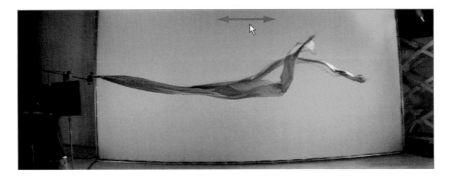

The green screen color appears in the screenColour swatch.

7   To view the alpha channel, position the pointer in the Viewer and press the A key.

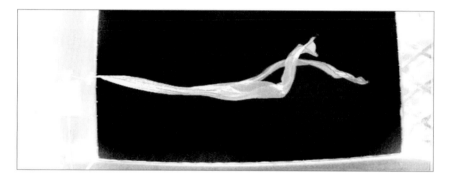

There are gray values in both the background and the foreground.

8   Try removing the gray values by adjusting the screenRange parameter to a value of *0.025*.

Raising the screenRange value increases the contrast in the mask, but adjusting it too high will result in the loss of fine detail. A second set of mask controls is located in the fineControl subtree. Raising or lowering the Gain parameters increases or decreases the mask in the shadow, midtone, or highlight areas.

9   Click the plus sign (+) next to fineControl to expand the fineControl subtree.

10 Set the midtoneGain parameter to *−0.175*.

The noise disappears in the foreground areas. The remaining background noise, in addition to the items on the stage, can be removed by creating a garbageMatte using a RotoShape node.

11 Switch from the Color Picker to the Node View tab.

12 Select a RotoShape node from the Image tab.

13 View the **scarf** clip while editing RotoShape1.

14 Set the Viewer to display the RGB channels and draw a shape around the scarf that approximates the following one.

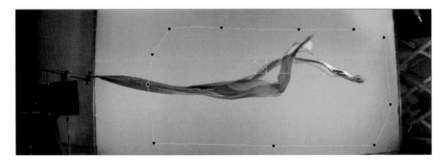

Normally, when you draw a garbageMatte, the shape surrounds the areas that you want to remove—hence the name. In this case, the shape should be inverted.

15 From the Color tab, add an Invert node after RotoShape1.

16 Connect the output of Invert1 to the fourth input (garbageMatte) of KeyLight1.

17 Double-click Keylight1 to view and edit its parameters

The garbageMatte has removed all extraneous items from the set, and the Viewer displays the composite. So far, so good.

Compositing Outside Keylight

When the foreground item within the green screen requires color adjustments or transformations, it's best to break the compositing out of the keying operations and use an Over node instead. To accomplish this, set the output to Unpremult (unpremultiplied). When selected, the key is knocked out of the foreground but then divided by its mask. This allows you to apply color corrections before compositing with an Over node.

> **NOTE ▶** If you are applying only filters or transforms, you can set the output parameter to On Black.

1 Set Output to Unpremult.

When the output is switched to Unpremult, the composite looks nasty. Don't worry; it's only temporary, until you composite with an Over node.

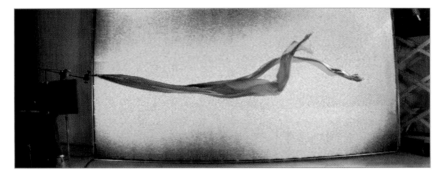

Next, use a Move2D node with an Over node to recomposite the background.

2   Insert a Move2D node after Keylight1.

The Move2D node is used for positioning the scarf.

3   From the Layer tab, add an Over node after Move2D1 and connect Stabilize1 to the right input.

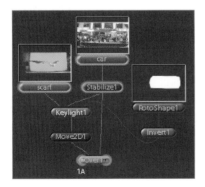

Here's where the magic happens:

4   In the Over1 parameters, activate preMultiply.

The unpremultiplied crap around the scarf is removed. Color correction and filtering nodes can now be placed between Keylight and Over1 without consequence.

Warping the Scarf

Even though the scarf is not connected to the woman's neck, you can probably tell that it won't look right—it's way too wide. You'll see what I mean once the scarf is positioned. We'll use warping to deform the scarf and make it much thinner.

Position the Scarf

1   View Over1 and edit the parameters of Move2D1.

2   Press the Control key and move your pointer over the center circle onscreen control until it highlights. When it highlights, drag and then release over the left end of the scarf.

This sets the center point for rotating and positioning the scarf.

3   Drag the Center crosshairs and release when they are positioned directly behind the woman's neck.

4   Rotate the scarf counterclockwise by setting the Angle parameter to a value of 5.

The scarf rotates upward, pivoting around the Center position.

5   Make a flipbook of what you have done so far.

It is obvious that the scarf is way too wide. Time for some warpage.

6   Close the flipbook.

Pinching the Scarf

A wide variety of image distortion and manipulation tasks are handled with the versatile Warper node. In this section, we'll use the Warper to pinch the scarf into a smaller, thinner shape.

1   Temporarily ignore the Move2D1 node by highlighting it and pressing the I key.

2 Select Keylight1 and choose a Warper node from the Warp tab.

3 Draw a square around the left end of the scarf by clicking the Viewer to add points.

As with the RotoShape node, click the first point to close the shape. (In fact, all the shape-drawing tools are identical to those in the RotoShape node.)

Each shape you create using the Warper node is yellow, indicating that it's unassigned and doesn't yet have any effect on the image. The next step is to create a corresponding target shape. Target shapes specify how the pixels defined by the source shape will be deformed. To create the actual warping effect, you connect the source to the target shape.

4   Deactivate the Shape Transform control. It just gets in the way.

5   Right-click the square shape and choose Duplicate and Connect Shape.

This duplicates and connects a source and target shape in a single step.

6   Click somewhere off the shape to deselect all points.

7   Hide the source shape by clicking on the Show Source Shapes icon in the Warper Viewer toolbar so you don't accidentally move its points.

8   Select the individual points and drag them until you have something that looks like the shape on the following page.

As you move the points, the image is warped based on the new point positions.

9   Make the source shape visible again so that you can see how it relates to the target shape.

Once connected, source shapes become light blue, target shapes become dark blue, and the connection lines between them become purple. Because the overallDisplacement parameter defaults to 1, the effect is immediately seen as the target shape's points are moved.

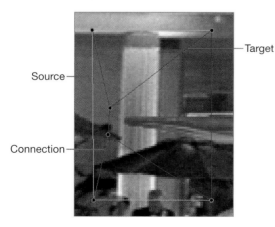

10 Make Move2D1 active again by highlighting it and pressing the I key.

11 Click the right side of Move2D1 to edit it.

12 Drag on the screen until the scarf aligns properly with the back of the woman's neck.

13 Create a flipbook.

The size of the scarf where it connects to the woman's neck looks natural now. The Warper was successfully used to push and pull the image's pixels into the desired shape. As far as the composite is concerned, there are color-matching problems, which you will tackle next.

14 Close the flipbook.

NOTE ▶ Shake can also morph images. The Morpher node blends two images together to create the effect of one transforming into another. The Morpher node does this by combining two warping operations, one to warp the source into the target shape and another to warp the target into the source shape. To achieve the illusion that the first image is changing into the second, a cross-fade dissolves from the first warp to the second.

Color-Correcting the Scarf

The color of the scarf is completely wrong. We'll use ColorReplace to change
the color, and we'll animate the brightness to match the lighting variations
in the images.

1   Select Move2D1 and insert a ColorReplace node from the Color tab.

ColorReplace allows you to isolate a color according to its hue, saturation,
and value, and replace it with a different color. Other areas of the spectrum will remain unchanged.

2   Make sure your Update mode is set to Always.

The Always Update mode will make it easier to choose the replacement color.

3   Also, make sure that your Time Bar is still set to frame 48.

4   Click the SourceColor swatch and drag over an area of the scarf.

5   Now click the ReplaceColor swatch and drag over the woman's shoulder until the color of the scarf matches that of the woman's dress.

As you drag on the woman's shoulder, the color of the scarf updates interactively because of the Always Update mode. The remaining gold areas on the scarf need to be tuned out.

6   Drag the satFalloff slider to about 0.6. The scarf will turn completely pink.

Now that we have a good color match, we can move on to correcting the brightness.

7   Set the Update mode to Release and drag the Time Bar to frame 1.

Look at the difference in brightness between the woman's head and the scarf.

8   Go to frame 15.

By frame 15, the brightness of the scarf has normalized. Using an Expand node and a few keyframes, you'll animate the scarf's brightness.

9   Switch from the Color Picker to the Node View.

10   Go back to frame 1 and, from the Color tab, add an Expand node after
Color Replace1.

Expand increases the amount of pure black and white in the image.

11   Activate the High Color keyframe icon.

The High Color parameter will increase the whites in the image.

12   Press the V key and drag left over the HighColor parameter until all three
values show 0.25. You may need to make repeated drags.

All right, it looks like hell. The scarf matches where it connects to the
woman's neck, but the rest of it is blown out. A little masking is in order.

13   From the Mask Create pull-down menu, choose RGrad.

An RGrad is automatically created and connected to the Mask input of the Expand1 node.

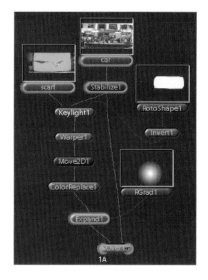

14 Position the crosshairs over the woman's head and adjust the inner and outer circle onscreen controls to limit the effect of the Expand1 node.

I set the radius to 20 and the falloffRadius to 155.

15 Go to frames 8, 10, and 15 and drag while pressing the V key until the scarf's brightness matches on each of these frames.

I used the following values:

Frame	Value
1	.25
8	.30
10	.40
15	.80

16 Make a flipbook.

Everything is finished except for restoring the original motion of the **car** clip.

17 Close the flipbook.

Destabilizing the Composite

In the beginning of the lesson, you stabilized the **car** clip so that it would be easier to add elements to the scene. Now that the shot is completed, let's add the motion from the **car** clip to the composite. I call this destabilization even though it is no different from a match move. You are just using the same tracking data originally used to stabilize the clip, but in a different way. If you invert the stabilization data, you get a match move.

1 Highlight the Over1 node and select a Stabilize node from the Transform tab.

> **NOTE ▶** For those of you using the full version of Shake, you can just copy and paste the Stabilize1 node using Command-C and Command-V and jump ahead to step 4. (The trial version of Shake included with this book does not allow you to copy and paste.)

2   Right-click track1 and select Load Track.

3   When the Select Track menu pops up, choose Stabilize1.track1 and
click OK.

Stabilize1.track1 is loaded into Stabilize2.track1.

4   Make applyTransform active and set inverseTransform to Match.

5   Make a flipbook.

All done.

6   Quit Shake.

Lesson Review

1.   Define warping.

2.   When is it best to break the compositing out of a keying operation?

3.   When you are adding elements to a moving image, what are your work-flow choices?

Answers

1.   Warping is a process that deforms a portion of an image.

2.   It is best to break the compositing out of a keying operation when the foreground item within the green screen requires color adjustments or transformations.

3.   When adding elements to a moving image, you could analyze the motion of the moving clip and apply that motion to your elements. Or, you could stabilize the moving clip, combine all your elements, and then destabilize the composite.

14

Lesson Files	APTS_Shake > Lessons > Lesson14
Media	bathroom.1-46.iff
	battle.iff
	bg.1-52.iff
	blob.1-46.iff
	bullet.1-52.iff
	jeans_comp.iff
	jean_fg.iff
	plane.1-30.iff
	smoke.1-52.iff
Time	This lesson takes approximately 1 hour to complete.
Goals	Use command-line Shake in the Terminal window
	Load single images and sequences into a flipbook
	Compare images
	Convert files
	Get help
	Get image information
	Execute command-line compositing

Lesson 14
The Command Line

This lesson shows you how to use Shake in the OS X Terminal program to launch flipbooks, perform file conversions, launch scripts, and generally execute any string of commands that are also available in the interface. I highly encourage you to learn the command-line syntax, because it often provides a much easier way to do certain tasks than firing up the interface.

You can use the command line to composite clips efficiently in Shake without launching the interface.

Shake in the Command Line

Every function that you can perform in the interface can also be executed in a Terminal window. The command line is perfect for when you know exactly (or almost exactly) what you want to do, and it's not very complicated. Its great benefit is speed. If you just want to use high-resolution images to make video-resolution copies with a change in color, typing that out in the command line may be easier than actually launching the interface and connecting all the nodes.

Common Command-Line Uses

▶ Resize, rotate, crop, or flip/flop images from film scans

▶ Add sharpening filters as you resize elements upward

▶ Change image file formats

▶ Place the luminance of an image into its alpha channel

▶ Load images into a flipbook for playback

▶ Render scripts

▶ Check a rendered, computer-generated element over a background plate

▶ Renumber and rename files

▶ Compare two images

Most importantly, you can also run commands remotely from the privacy of your own home—even sitting in your underwear. When you log in to your office in the middle of the night, you'll really love that Shake has an expansive command-line feature set.

Some Useful Unix Commands

Unix is a popular multiuser, multitasking operating system. Originally designed in the early 1970s to be used only by programmers, Unix is known for its cryptic commands and general lack of user-friendliness.

Though you would never know it, Mac OS X is based on Unix. You can run and execute Unix commands as well as Shake command-line functions in the OS X Terminal program. So getting familiar with some of the more common Unix commands is a good idea. Here are a few that you'll find useful:

cd

▶   cd changes the current working directory to a new directory. If you don't specify anything after typing cd, you will change directories to your home directory.

▶   Usage: cd [*directory*]

Options:

    ▶   ../ : Takes you up one directory.

    ▶   ../.. : Takes you up two directories.

    ▶   ../../.. : Takes you up three directories. You get the idea.

    NOTE ▶ In Unix, using correct syntax is important. For example, cd ../ will take you up one directory level, but cd.. (no space) will return cd..: Command not found.

cp

▶   cp copies a file or files to a specified directory under the same name. If the destination file exists, it will be overwritten.

▶   Usage: cp file1 file2 or cp –r files directory

Options:

    ▶   –r: Copies a directory and all its contents.

ls

▶   ls lists the files contained in the current or specified directory.

▶   Usage: ls [*options*] [*directory*]

Options:

▶ –a: Lists all files including "." or hidden files.

▶ –l: Long-format listing.

▶ –lrt: Long-format listing in reverse chronological order. This is good for showing the last set of files recorded in a directory.

mv

▶ mv moves a file or directory to a new name or location.

▶ Usage: mv *file target*

rm

▶ rm deletes one or more files.

▶ Usage: rm [*options*] *files*

Options:

▶ –r: Removes a directory and all its contents.

Loading a Single Image

Ready or not, let's use Shake in the command line.

1 Open the Terminal program, located in the Applications/Utilities folder.

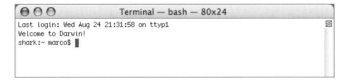

```
Terminal — bash — 80x24
Last login: Wed Aug 24 21:31:58 on ttyp1
Welcome to Darwin!
shark:~ marco$
```

2 Navigate to the Lesson14 folder using the cd command. If you copied the Lessons folder directly to your Macintosh hard drive using the instructions in the Getting Started section of this book, type *cd APTS_Shake/Lessons/Lesson14* and press Enter.

NOTE ▶ You must press the Enter key on the keyboard to execute command-line functions.

Instead of typing out every letter of a file or folder, you can use the file-completion shortcut in the Terminal window: whenever you press the Tab key, a list will show you all potential files that match what you type.

3   Type *shake batt* and press the Tab key.

This will list **battle.iff** for you.

4   Press Enter.

The **battle** clip is shown in a Viewer.

You can see the image name and resolution in the title bar.

5   Drag the left mouse button over the image to see the *X-Y* coordinate and the red, green, blue, and alpha values in the title bar.

Shake measures the image starting in the bottom-left corner at 0,0. This means that the right edge will be the width of the image minus 1. The same goes for the top of the image.

Here are some of the things that you can do in the Viewer:

▶   Zoom in on the image with the – and = keys near the Delete key.

▶   Pan the image using the right mouse button.

▶   Center the image and remove all zooming by pressing the Home key.

▶   View the red, green, blue, and alpha channels by pressing the R, G, B, or A keys. To go back to full color, press C.

▶   Close the image by pressing Esc.

6   Close the battle.iff flipbook.

NOTE ▶ When you are done with each command line, close the flipbook so you can move on to the next step.

To view more than one image, enter multiple filenames.

7   Type *shake plane.0001.iff bg.0001.iff*

Two flipbooks open, but you see only one, as they are placed one on top of the other.

8   Drag the title bar of **bg.0001.iff** to the side so you can see **plane.0001.iff**.

9   Close all flipbooks.

> **TIP** ▸ You can repeat previous commands by using the up arrow key on the command line. Each time you press it, it will list the previous command, stepping back through your history. Use the left and right arrow keys to change portions of the command. Pressing the down arrow key will take you to the next command in your history list.

Loading a Sequence

Loading a sequence of images is just like loading a single image, except that you give a frame range and put a marker in the input filename that represents where the frames are. The marker can handle unpadded or padded frame numbers (for example, image.1 or image.0001). If you want padded frames, use #. For unpadded frames, use @. You can also use printlike formatting, such as %d, %04d, and so on. Finally, you may use an arbitrary number of @ signs for padding other than four digits.

Here are some examples:

Shake Format	Reads/Writes
image.#.iff	image.0001.iff, image.0002.iff
image.%04d.iff	image.0001.iff, image.0002.iff
image.@.iff	image.1.iff, image.2.iff
image.%d.iff	image.1.iff, image.2.iff
image.@@@.iff	image.001.iff, image.002.iff
image.%3d.iff	image.001.iff, image.002.iff

1   To load **plane.0001.iff** through **plane.0030.iff**, type *shake plane.#.iff –t 1–30*

The –t flag in the command line stands for *time* and specifies the frame range of your sequence.

You should have 30 frames loaded in a flipbook.

2   To play the images, press . (the > key).

3   To play backward, press , (the < key).

4   To stop playing, press the spacebar.

Here are some other things you can do with a flipbook:

▶ Step through the animation by pressing the left and right arrow keys.

▶ Scrub through the animation by pressing Shift and clicking the left mouse button.

▶ Ping-pong the playback by pressing Shift->.

▶ Play through once by pressing Control->.

▶ Increase or decrease the frame rate by pressing the + or – keys on the numeric keypad.

NOTE ▶ The frame rate is displayed on the title bar. If you are getting real-time playback, it will say "Locked."

▶ Play back in real time by pressing the T key. This will drop frames if Shake can't maintain the desired speed. If Shake drops frames, it will tell you what percent is being dropped.

Using the –t option to describe your frame range is an extremely flexible way to look at any variety or order of images.

5 Close the flipbook.

6 Type *shake plane.#.iff –t 1–30x2*

   Only odd frames—1, 3, 5, and so on—are loaded into the flipbook.

7 Step through the clip with the arrow keys.

   On the title bar, notice how the name of the clip updates showing every other frame.

8 Close the flipbook.

Comparing Images

You can load two images simultaneously into a flipbook to compare them.

1   Type *shake jeans_fg.iff –compare jeans_comp.iff*

2   To compare the images, press Control–Shift–left mouse button and slide back and forth inside the flipbook.

You can also:

▶   Switch the compare buffers by pressing S.

▶   Toggle the vertical and horizontal splits by pressing V and H.

▶   Fade between the images by pressing F.

What's cool here is that the compare function works with moving images.

3   Close the flipbook.

Converting Files

So far, you have been loading images into a flipbook, without putting an output file in the command line. To convert an image to a different file, merely add an output filename following the –fileout command.

1   Type *shake battle.iff –fileout battle_cry.jpg*

    or

2   Type *shake battle.iff –fo battle_cry.jpg*

    This writes *battle.iff* as the JPEG image **battle_cry.jpg**.

    If you want to convert an entire sequence, use the -t flag.

3   Type *shake –v battle.#.iff –fo battle.@.rgb –t 1–30*

    This will write battle.0001.iff as **battle.1.rgb**, up to frame 30. The @ sign sits in as the unpadded frame number symbol. Since you used the –v (verbose) flag, Shake shows you how long each frame takes to render.

    Shake never makes explicit changes to the data in an image based on the file format that is being used. Thus, there would be no automatic log-to-linear conversion if you were to convert from the Cineon file format. To make such a conversion, include a delogc command.

Getting Help

As you may suspect, there are a lot of Shake commands that you can execute in the Terminal window. There are a few methods (other than reading the Shake User Manual) for getting help in the command line. First of all, to figure out a command, you can type *shake –help command_name*.

1   Type *shake –help delogc*

    In the Terminal window, Shake gives you the syntax for the delogc command:

    –delogc [rOffset] [gOffset] [bOffset] [black] [white] [nGamma] [dGamma] [softClip]

```
 ● ● ●              Terminal — bash — 80x24
shark:DVD/Lessons/Lesson14 marco$ shake -help delogc
    -delogc         [rOffset] [gOffset] [bOffset] [black] [white] [nGamma]
                    [dGamma] [softClip]
```

You can also get general help on a concept, such as multiplying.

2 Type *shake –help mul*

Shake returns the following output in the Terminal window:

–imult

–mmult

–mult

–multilayer

–multiplane

–multiply

```
● ○ ○            Terminal — bash — 80x24
shark:DVD/Lessons/Lesson14 marco$ shake -help mul
   -imult          <background> [clipMode] [percent] [ignoreZero]
   -mmult          [ignoreZero]
   -mult           [red] [green] [blue] [alpha] [depth]
   -multilayer     <version> <clipLayer> <postMatteMult> [...]
   -multiplane     [version] [serializedPlugins] [clipLayer]
                   [postMatteMult] [autoOrder] [addDefaultCameras]
                   [renderCamera] [numCameras] [numCloudPoints]
                   [viewerMode] [hideCamOSC] [camPathVisible] [sceneScale]
                   [cameraName] [cameraFocalLength] [xCameraTranslate]
                   [yCameraTranslate] [zCameraTranslate] [xCameraRotate]
                   [yCameraRotate] [zCameraRotate] [cameraRotateOrder]
                   [cameraFilmBackWidth] [cameraFilmBackHeight]
                   [cameraScale] [fitResolution] [fitOffset] [xFilmOffset]
                   [yFilmOffset] [useDevAspect] [devAspect] [xFilter]
                   [yFilter] [motionBlur] [shutterTiming] [shutterOffset]
                   [isDefaultCamera] [interestDistance] [numViewerPanes]
                   [viewer1Cam] [xPan1] [yPan1] [zoom1] [viewer2Cam]
                   [xPan2] [yPan2] [zoom2] [viewer3Cam] [xPan3] [yPan3]
                   [zoom3] [viewer4Cam] [xPan4] [yPan4] [zoom4] [...]
   -multiply       <background> [clipMode]
```

3 If you would like to see a complete list of commands, type *shake –help*

This displays a list of every single Shake command, as well as any macros that you created.

```
● ○ ○            Terminal — bash — 80x24
   -vtrin          [autoAlpha] [deInterlacing] [tcm] [in] [out] [duration]
                   [reel] [clip] [...]
   -vtrout         [tcm] [in] [out] [duration] [yuvEncode] [...]
   -vv
   -vwipe          [i2] [blur] [reverse] [mixPercent]
   -warper         [version] [displayImage] [overallDisplacement]
                   [addBorderShape] [overSampling] [state] [dodPad] [...]
   -warpx          [oversamping] [xExpr] [yExpr] [xDelta] [yDelta]
   -window         [left] [bottom] [right] [top]
   -xor            <background> [clipMode] [useMatte]
   -yiqtorgb
   -yuvtorgb
   -z              <scale>
   -zblur          [amount] [near] [far] [focusCenter] [focusRange] [steps]
                   [stepBlend]
```

Getting Image Info

Shake can quickly get information about an image with the –info command. If you are using this option, it will not pop the image into a flipbook but instead will give you a text output in the Terminal window:

1   Type *shake battle.iff –info*

In the shell window, you'll see the following:

Filename: battle.iff

Type: RGBA

Size: 478x560

Depth: 8 bits

Z-Buffer: none

Format: Shake

It gives you lots of info that is pretty self-explanatory. If you change the parameters, the –info command will reflect this.

2   Type *shake battle.iff –zoom 2 –bytes 2 –reorder rgbn –info*

In the shell window, you'll see the following:

Filename: battle.iff

Type: RGB

Size: 956x1120

Depth: 16 bits

Z-Buffer: none

Format: Shake

I zoomed up the image with –zoom, which gives me a higher resolution. I also put in 2 bytes per channel, which gives me a bit depth of 16 bits, and I stripped out the alpha channel (n in the –reorder option means no channel), leaving a three-channel image. Shake doesn't process the image unless you use a –fileout command followed by an output image.

Basic Command-Line Compositing

Basic compositing on the command line can be very useful, especially for testing composites. Let's start by viewing the elements.

1   Type *shake bg.#.iff –t 1–52* and play the clip when it is done loading.

  This is the live-action background plate.

2   Close the flipbook when you are finished looking at it.

3   Make flipbooks of the **bullet.1-52.iff** and **smoke.1-52.iff** clips and play them.

  The bullet and smoke clips are computer-generated elements that you'll composite with the background.

4   Close all open flipbooks.

5   Type *shake bullet.#.iff –over bg.#.iff –t 1–52* and play the composite when it is done loading.

The bullet is composited over the background and looks pretty good, but you still need to add the smoke.

6   Type *shake smoke.#.iff –over bullet.#.iff –over bg.#.iff –t 1–52*

The bullet and smoke have been composited very quickly. This is a great way to test your elements without wasting any time.

7   Close the flipbook.

Are you feeling pretty cocky right now? If so, you're ready for the next step. Let's raise the bar and try a more complicated command-line composite.

Command-Line Compositing, in Depth

This section demonstrates the different degrees to which the command line can be used, starting simply as a flipbook and gradually adding complexity up to a full-blown script. OK, I admit, this stuff is pretty boring, but somebody has got to explain it. Once you get past a certain point, your best bet is to move to the Shake graphical interface.

We'll start by playing the computer-generated element, and progressively work it onto a composite.

1   Type *shake blob.#.iff –t 1–46*

    This loads up the element for playback.

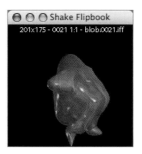

    To place it over a larger background, just use the –over command:

2   Type *shake blob.#.iff –over bathroom.#.iff –t 1–46*

3   Play the flipbook.

    The blob doesn't appear to be positioned properly, so let's move it to a better position with the –pan command. But you say to yourself, "Self, I don't know the usage parameter for the –pan command." That's OK, because all you need to do is use the –help command.

4   Type *shake –help pan*

    Two commands are listed: –pan and –expand.

    For the –pan command, we're only interested in the first two parameters, xPan and yPan.

5   Type *shake blob.#.iff –pan 85 40 –over bathroom.#.iff –t 1–46*

6   Now look at the above image's alpha channel by pressing the A key.

You can see that the bathroom has a previously created mask around the inside of the door. We can use this mask to put the blob guy inside the bathroom by using an –inside command before the –over.

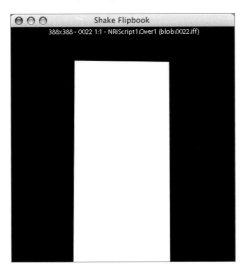

7 Type *shake blob.#.iff –pan 85 40 –inside bathroom.#.iff –over bathroom.#.iff –t 1–46*

The blob is placed inside the bathroom behind the door frame, but it needs a shadow. Next, we are going to add a really fake shadow.

8 Type *shake blob.#.iff –pan 85 40 –addshadow –33 –20 30 0 0 0 .6 –inside bathroom.#.iff –over bathroom.#.iff –t 1–46*

If you feel the need to know the command usage for –addshadow, you can use the –help command.

How about a little color correction? Maybe the blob should be a sickening green color. You can do this with a –reorder command by substituting the green channel for the red channel.

9 Type *shake blob.#.iff –pan 85 40 –reorder gbga –addshadow –33 –20 30 0 0 0 .6 –inside bathroom.#.iff –over bathroom.#.iff –t 1–46*

Make the blob even greener by using a -mult command.

10 Type *shake blob.#.iff –pan 85 40 –reorder gbga –mult 1 1.2 .6 1 1 –addshadow –33 –20 30 0 0 0 .6 –inside bathroom.#.iff –over bathroom.#.iff –t 1–46*

At this point, the command line is getting pretty ridiculous. So append –gui at the end of it. This will create a process tree in the interface, allowing you to continue the composite in a more civilized environment.

11 Type *shake blob.#.iff –pan 85 40 –reorder gbga –mult 1 1.2 .6 1 1 –addshadow –33 –20 30 0 0 0 .6 –inside bathroom.#.iff –over bathroom.#.iff –t 1–46 –gui*

Shake automatically creates a tree from your command-line entries.

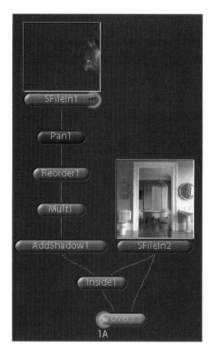

The Shake interface is for wimps. Quick, exit before anybody sees you.

12 Quit the Shake interface.

Launching Scripts from the Command Line

The most efficient way to do loads of rendering is by batch-rendering a script, since you don't need to fire up the interface. All you need to do is navigate to the location of one of your scripts and type *shake –v –exec my_cool_script.shk* (where *my_cool_script.shk* is a script that you create). The –exec command executes all FileOuts in the script. Each frame is rendered in turn, and since you typed –v, Shake shows you in the Terminal window which frame it is working on and how long each frame takes to render.

Welcome to the fabulous world of command-line Shake. You will no doubt be able to impress your friends with your newfound knowledge.

> **NOTE** ▶ The saving of scripts is disabled in the trial version of Shake.

Lesson Review

1. What can command-line Shake do for you?

2. What will your output filename look like if you specify test.#.rgb in the fileout?

3. How can you see a complete list of commands?

Answers

1. Command-line Shake lets you do such things as render scripts, load images into a flipbook, and change image file formats—all without firing up the Shake interface.

2. If you specify the fileout to be test.#.rgb, your file output will be test.0001.rgb.

3. To see a complete list of commands, type *shake –help* in the Terminal window.

Final Cut Studio Workflows

Apple's professional audio and video applications are designed to work together seamlessly, even in the most demanding postproduction workflows. The Final Cut Studio product line—a comprehensive and integrated postproduction package—comprises Final Cut Pro 5, Soundtrack Pro, Motion 2, DVD Studio Pro 4, Compressor 2, LiveType 2, and Cinema Tools 3. These tools, in conjunction with Shake 4 and Logic Pro 7, provide professional editors with the most comprehensive toolkit in the industry.

The appendix, on the DVD accompanying this book, details the roles of each application in the production process. You will also find a sample Final Cut Studio workflow and information on "roundtripping," the ability to embed and open project files while working in another application. See Lessons > **x_Appendix-Final Cut Studio Workflows**.

Glossary

3:2 pull-down A technique to convert film footage to video footage and back again.

AIFF Short for Audio Interchange File Format, an 8-bit sound file format developed by Apple.

alpha channel In color images, the fourth channel after the red, green, and blue channels. In black-and-white images, the second channel after the luminance channel.

animation The process of creating imagery on a frame-by-frame basis either by hand or digitally.

Audio Panel A tool used to read in AIFF or WAV files, mix them together, extract animation curves based on the audio frequency, and manipulate the timing of the sound.

blue screen An evenly lit, bright, pure blue background used behind images when they're filmed. The compositing process then replaces all the blue in the picture with another image. Sometimes also called green screen when the screen that is used is green.

Channel Viewer Toggles between the full-color image and the alpha channel.

chroma-keying Electronically matting or inserting an image from one camera into the picture produced by another. The subject to be inserted is shot against a solid color background, and signals from the two sources are then merged.

color correction Any process that alters the perceived color of an image.

color matching Making the color of one shot correspond with that of another.

Color Picker A tool that allows you to sample colors from the Viewer and transfer the color settings to applicable parameters.

compositing Creating an image by combining two or more images.

concatenation The process of mathematically combining multiple color corrections into one.

Curve Editor A tool that allows you to create, view, and modify keyframes as well as animation curves and audio waveforms.

D

dustbusting The process of painting dirt off an image.

F

File Browser An interactive tool for tracking files or for navigating through the network to load or write scripts, images, lookup files, and expressions.

FileIn The node used to read images into Shake.

FileOut The node used to save images.

filter A function that transforms an image in some manner, such as a blur filter.

flipbook A RAM-based image player that loads a clip into memory so that it can be played back in real time.

four-point tracking A process traditionally used to match the perspective of one shot and apply it to another—for instance, tracking the four corners of a sign and replacing it with a new billboard.

Frame stroke mode A mode used to paint only on the current frame.

function See nodes.

G

garbage matte A matte that removes unwanted objects from an image.

Globals parameters Parameters that affect the behavior of an entire effect setup.

interlacing The manner in which a television picture is composed, scanning alternate lines of two video fields to create one frame every one-thirtieth of a second in NTSC.

Interpolate stroke mode A mode that interpolates brushstrokes between chosen frames.

keyframe A value set at various frames of an animation. Keyframes transition from one to another over time.

knot A point on an animation curve or shape.

Kodak Cineon A 10-bit logarithmic file format that uses an efficient color compression scheme based on the idea that the human eye is more sensitive to shadows and midtones than to highlights.

macros The combination of multiple functions into a new function. They let you control what parameters are exposed and hide parameters that don't need to be changed.

mask An image or a part of an image usually used to limit or constrain an effect.

matte An image that controls the opacity of another image.

motion tracking A technique that involves selecting a particular region of an image and analyzing its motion over time.

multipass compositing The process of separating scenes into multiple layers, allowing flexibility in the manipulation and adjustment of the various layers.

MultiPlane compositing The process of compositing 2D layers in a 3D space. A virtual camera, similar to those found in 3D animation packages, controls the view of the output image. This camera can be animated by keyframing parameters or by importing 3D camera and tracking data from third-party programs.

Node workspace The Shake workspace where clips and functions, as represented by nodes, are combined and connected into a process tree.

nodes The image manipulation commands used in Shake.

noodle A line connecting nodes on a process tree.

NTSC National Television Standards Committee, which developed the color-transmission system used in the United States. Consists of 525 lines scanned at 30 frames per second.

O

offset tracking A tracking process that is used when your reference pattern becomes obscured. With offset tracking, the track point follows the same path, but a new search region/reference pattern is used to acquire the tracking data.

on-the-fly proxy A proxy that is generated only when needed and discarded when your disk is full.

P

PAL Phase Alternation by Line. The color-transmission system used in many European countries. Consists of 625 lines scanned at a rate of 25 frames per second.

Parameters workspace The Shake workspace where parameters for a node are adjusted.

Persist stroke mode A mode in which brushstrokes persist from frame to frame.

point cloud A series of tracked points that follow along with features in the image.

premultiplication The process of multiplying the RGB channels in an image by their alpha channel.

Primatte A process used to extract a single color background from an image and create a transparency matte that allows the user to put the extracted foreground onto a different background.

process tree A treelike structure comprising interconnected images and processes such as color corrections, layering commands, and keying functions, among others.

proxy A lower-resolution copy that you substitute for your high-resolution images.

Proxy button A button used to activate the use of proxy resolutions.

proxy ratio Determines the size relationship of the proxy to the original file.

reference pattern The inner box of a tracker. It defines a small pattern that will be searched for in subsequent frames.

R

render To convert an image into a fully formed 3D image.

resolution The quality of an image, measured in pixels per inch.

RGB channel The combination of the red, green, and blue channels of an image.

roto A frame-by-frame shape-drawing technique to create animated shapes over time.

rotoscoping A frame-by-frame hand-painting technique to create imagery over time.

script A text file that contains all of the information about your process tree. The script can be loaded into the interface for further modification.

S

scrub The action of shuttling quickly through an image sequence.

search region The outer box of a tracker, which should be the maximum amount your tracking point will move between frames.

stabilization The process of selecting a particular region of an image and analyzing its motion over time. Once analyzed, the motion data is inverted and applied to the clip, causing it to become stable. Clips need to be stabilized for a variety of reasons, from weave created by an unsteady camera gate to a shaky camera move.

thumbnail A small preview version of an image.

T

Time Bar An interface element that displays a time range in Shake.

tool tabs Tabbed windows in the Shake interface where all the tools are conveniently located.

tracker A node that analyzes the motion of a clip.

tracking The process of analyzing the motion of one clip and applying that motion to another clip.

track point The center cross in a tracker. It represents the position of the motion track.

transform control A control that allows you manipulate an image using parameters such as pan, scale, and rotate.

V

Viewer A display tool for viewing images.

vignette A popular photographic effect in which the photo gradually darkens around the edges, usually in an oval shape.

W

warping A process in which a portion of an image is deformed. The warp effect can be an animation over time or a static adjustment that occurs over the entire shot. It can be used to make animals talk, enhance facial expressions, or cause body parts to shrink or expand.

WAV A sound file format developed by Microsoft and IBM.

woof An expression that can be yelled with gusto to indicate that a control or setting has hit its perfect mark.

Index

The Apple Pro Training Series

Apple Pro Training Series: Final Cut Pro 5
0-321-33481-7

In this best-selling guide, Diana Weynand starts with basic video editing techniques and takes you all the way through Final Cut Pro's powerful advanced features. Using world-class documentary footage, you'll learn to mark and edit clips, color correct sequences, create transitions, apply filters and effects, add titles, work with audio, and more.

Apple Pro Training Series: Advanced Editing Techniques in Final Cut Pro 5
0-321-33549-X

Director and editor Michael Wohl shares must-know professional techniques for cutting dialogue scenes, action scenes, fight and chase scenes, documentaries, comedy, music videos, multi-camera projects, and more. Also covers Soundtrack Pro, audio finishing, managing clips and media, and working with film.

Apple Pro Training Series: Advanced Color Correction and Effects in Final Cut Pro 5
0-321-33548-1

This Apple-authorized guide delivers hard-to-find training in real-world color correction and effects techniques, including motion effects, keying and compositing, titling, scene-to-scene color matching, and correcting for broadcast specifications.

Apple Pro Training Series: Optimizing Your Final Cut Pro System
0-321-26871-7

Written and field-tested by industry pros Sean Cullen, Matthew Geller, Charles Roberts, and Adam Wilt, this is the ultimate guide for installing, configuring, optimizing, and trouble-shooting Final Cut Pro in real-world post-production environments.

Apple Pro Training Series: Final Cut Pro for Avid Editors
0-321-24577-6

Master trainer Diana Weynand takes you through a comprehensive "translation course" designed for professional video and film editors who already know their way around Avid nonlinear systems.

Apple Pro Training Series: Getting Started with Final Cut Studio
0-321-36991-2

This Apple-authorized guide provides newcomers with an ex-cellent overview of all products in Final Cut Studio: Final Cut Pro 5, Motion 2, Soundtrack Pro and DVD Studio Pro 4.

Apple Pro Train-ing Series: Final Cut Express HD
0-321-33533-3

The only Apple-authorized guide to Final Cut Express HD, this book delivers the techniques you need to make movie magic from the comfort of your Mac.

Apple Pro Training Series: Xsan 2/E
0-321-43232-0

Apple's exciting new enterprise-class file system offers high-speed access to centralized shared data. This handy booklet provides invaluable setup, configuration, and troubleshooting tips.

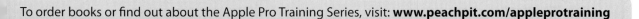

Apple Pro Training Series: DVD Studio Pro 4
0-321-33482-5

Learn to author professional interactive DVDs with this best-selling guide.

Apple Pro Training Series: Shake 4
0-321-25609-3

Apple-certified guide uses stunning real world sequences to reveal the wizardry of Shake 4.

Apple Pro Training Series: Shake 4 Quick Reference Guide
0-321-38246-3

Compact reference guide to Apple's leading compositing software.

Apple Pro Training Series: Getting Started with Motion
0-321-30533-7

Apple-certified guide makes sophisticated motion graphics accessible to newcomers.

Apple Pro Training Series: Motion
0-321-27826-7

Comprehensive guide to Apple's revolutionary motion graphics software.

Encyclopedia of Visual Effects
0-321-30334-2

Ultimate recipe book for visual effects artists working in Shake, Motion and Adobe After Effects.

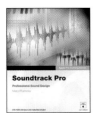

Apple Pro Training Series: Soundtrack Pro
0-321-35757-4

Create original soundtrack's with Apple's exciting new sound design software.

Apple Pro Training Series: Logic Pro 7 and Logic Express 7
0-321-25614-X

Create, mix, and polish your musical creations using Apple's pro audio software.

Apple Pro Training Series: Advanced Logic Pro 7
0-321-25607-7

Comprehensive guide takes you through Logic's powerful advanced features.

Apple Pro Training Series: Color Management with Mac OS X
0-321-24576-8

Project-based guide shows how to set up real-world color management workflows.

Apple Pro Training Series: Getting Started with Aperture
0-321-42275-9

Introduction to Apple's revolutionary workflow tool for professional photographers.

Apple Pro Training Series: Aperture
0-321-42276-7

Comprehensive book-DVD combo takes you step by step all the way through Aperture.

The Apple Training Series

Designed for system administrators, IT professionals, AppleCare technicians, and Mac enthusiasts, the Apple Training Series is both a self-paced learning tool and the official curriculum of the Apple Training and Certification program. For more information, go to **http://train.apple.com.**

Apple Training Series: Mac OS X Support Essentials
0-321-33547-3

Apple Training Series: Mac OS X Server Essentials
0-321-35758-2

Apple Training Series: Desktop and Portable Systems, Second Edition
0-321-33546-5

Apple Training Series: iWork '06
0-321-44225-3

Apple Training Series: Mac OS X System Administration Guide, Volume 1
0-321-36984-X

Apple Training Series: Mac OS X System Administration Guide, Volume 2
0-321-42315-1

Apple Training Series: iLife '06
0-321-42164-7

Apple Training Series: GarageBand 3
0-321-42165-5